How the Internet of Things Is Changing Our Colleges, Our Classrooms, and Our Students

How the Internet of Things Is Changing Our Colleges, Our Classrooms, and Our Students

Mickey Slimp
Roy Bartels

ROWMAN & LITTLEFIELD
Lanham • Boulder • New York • London

Published by Rowman & Littlefield
An imprint of The Rowman & Littlefield Publishing Group, Inc.
4501 Forbes Boulevard, Suite 200, Lanham, Maryland 20706
www.rowman.com

6 Tinworth Street, London, SE11 5AL, United Kingdom

British Library Cataloguing in Publication Information Available

Library of Congress Cataloging-in-Publication Data

Names: Slimp, Mickey, 1954– author. | Bartels, Roy, 1950– author.
Title: How the Internet of things is changing our colleges, our classrooms, and our students / Mickey Slimp, Roy Bartels.
Description: Lanham, Maryland : Rowman & Littlefield, [2019] | Includes bibliographical references and index.
Identifiers: LCCN 2018045174 (print) | LCCN 2018059075 (ebook) | ISBN 9781475842999 (electronic) | ISBN 9781475842975 (cloth : alk. paper) | ISBN 9781475842982 (pbk. : alk. paper)
Subjects: LCSH: Education, Higher—Effect of technological innovations on. | Internet in higher education. | Ubiquitous computing.
Classification: LCC LB2395.7 (ebook) | LCC LB2395.7 .S5 2019 (print) | DDC 378.1/758—dc23
LC record available at https://lccn.loc.gov/2018045174

∞™ The paper used in this publication meets the minimum requirements of American National Standard for Information Sciences—Permanence of Paper for Printed Library Materials, ANSI/NISO Z39.48-1992.

Printed in the United States of America

To Wayne Wedemeyer and Walt Magnussen, who helped jumpstart my adventures in networking and the Internet and to the many pioneers of distance learning in the Instructional Technology Council who showed me how to use the technology. I include Rodger Poole, Pamela Quinn, Michael Catchpole, Ray Pirkl, Ronda Edwards, and Jim Picquet.—M.S.

Contents

Foreword

To be honest, I have been somewhat frustrated with available information about the Internet of Things—especially as it relates to its anticipated role and overall impact for higher education. As might be expected, existing literature tends to focus more broadly on the impact on corporations and the overall lifestyle changes for the general population.

This book is exactly what all of us have been waiting for. Mickey Slimp and Roy Bartels provide the reader with all of the pertinent information needed to understand the Internet of Things: the fundamentals, the evolution in technologies, and long-needed discussion of the ultimate impact of this emerging trend on higher education.

To date, colleges and universities have been lagging in the necessary exploration and implementation strategies needed to support related Internet of Things technologies on their campuses. This book contains the information and understanding of the subject needed to inaugurate a transformative discussion. The data and case studies as well as the extensive professional experience of the authors will resonate with senior administrators, frontline practitioners, and faculty. It is a "must" read *before* you have that important discussion on campus. The book will then become a blueprint of sorts for exactly how your campus will move forward both in terms of technical support as well as in instruction.

As someone whose career has been primarily at the community college level, I am especially interested in the approach the book has taken. Community colleges play a special role in helping populations that have had little or no exposure to technology learn how to embrace technological evolution. This book provides the first opportunity I've encountered to better understand the nuances of the Internet of Things and empowers the reader to be able to identify how it is restructuring the educational environment. As you can imagine, raising interest in this topic at community colleges can be a challenge, but again the knowledge base of the book, coupled with its clarity of explanation and context, will be of great use to recruit change-agents in administration and instruction.

The book is also of great benefit for university professionals. More progress has been made in general awareness and the importance of the Internet of Things, but the authors' unbiased assessment and the extremely useful case studies will add greatly to the effort to support this critical set of emerging technologies. Universities have already been very active in the exploration of this emerging trend but mostly from a vendor-based perspective. Without a particular agenda, Slimp and Bartels are focused on providing a lucid, systematic review and assessment of the Internet of Things and its effect on learning. Clearly, this book is a refreshing change of pace from what has been available on the subject.

The overall approach of the book is designed to introduce the reader to the evolving nature of technology with an enticing "where we started/where we are/where we are going" theme to the topic of changing technologies in education. The authors use relevant data, case studies, and even brief stories to frame the evolution of technologies leading to the Internet of Things. Each chapter builds on the previous chapter and creates a cohesive and sound understanding of what the Internet of Things is and specifically how it is already impacting higher education and the classroom. This is news we can use; the Internet of Things is one of the least understood topics on your campus today. This book ensures the reader will have a deeper understanding of the transformation that is underway.

Ultimately, the Internet of Things will have a greater impact on education, our economy, and our lives than any other technological development we have experienced. This book is a must-read for anyone who serves as an opinion leader or change agent at his or her campus as well as for those wanting to know—and understand—the transformation that is already well underway. This book repeatedly reaffirms this transformation, with a focus on the practical applications of instructional technologies related to the rapidly expanding world of the Internet of Things.

In my view, of greatest value is the exploration of how education needs to change to better prepare our students for the 21st-century realities of profound technological transformation. The authors' strategy of imagining what the world will look like within 10 years allows the reader to better understand where our current approach to learning fails the student—and fails to prepare that student to be successful in the decades ahead. The book is engaging and informative for what could be a rather unengaging topic (technology). It's the kind of book you will find yourself quoting and referencing—just because the book's information and arguments are so contemporary.

ABOUT THE AUTHORS

I've known Mickey Slimp for more than 12 years, starting with his return to the board of directors for the Instructional Technology Council (ITC) in 2006. Of course, I had already heard about Mickey. He had served a previous number of terms as a board member and even as chair of the ITC. Mickey has always been a magical mix of visionary and pragmatist. He offers a contrast of simultaneously being able to see the "big picture" as well as the process and infrastructure needed to support it. That special ability is ever present in this book and gives the reader a broader and deeper understanding of the Internet of Things. In addition, Mickey is a special blend of administrator and academic. His understanding of curriculum and the role of technology benefits from his vast administrative experience managing a very large regional IT (information technology) network including K–12, hospitals, and higher education institutions in northeast Texas.

I met Roy Bartels at about the same time that I met Mickey—when Roy also joined the Instructional Technology Council Board of Directors. Roy is a published author, with a first love of writing fiction. He is also a very experienced administrator in the fields of IT and distance learning. Like Mickey, he too is a pragmatist and looks for the practical applications of technology in education and related fields. Roy has a strong level of experience from the campus perspective and has had ground level experience in the adoption of new technologies as well as the challenges of technology deployment.

As a political scientist, futurist, distance learning administrator, and tenured faculty member, I can see both the politics and the transformative value of technology not only in education but, literally, in every aspect of our lives. For more than 20 years, I have stayed active in efforts to better inform national legislators and regulators regarding the imperative need to support a rapid expansion of online learning and the virtual learning environment at America's colleges and universities.

Fred Lokken

Chair, Instructional Technology Council (an Affiliated Council of the American Association of Community Colleges)

Author, the annual *Trends in eLearning: Tracking the Impact of eLearning at Community Colleges*

Tenured Professor of Political Science, Truckee Meadows Community College

Member, Forward50, National Leadership Higher Education Committee of 50 (www.forward-50.org)

Executive Commissioner, Nevada Western Interstate Commission of Higher Education

Acknowledgments

The first acknowledgment for the creation of this book goes to Roy Bartels. As a coauthor, Roy knew just when to jump in and to add the right amount of technology to keep the pages rolling. Thank you as well to the many contributors who provided case studies, examples, photos, and interviews to expand our story. Likewise, Sarah Jubar, our editor at Rowman & Littlefield, was just right in providing both the leeway and the prods at the right times to bring this to closure.

In addition, from the Instructional Technology Council (ITC), Fred Lokken, Carol Spalding, and Jean Runyon for encouraging Roy and me to focus on the idea of the Internet of Things. A number of the ideas in the book were incubated in and case studies generated from ITC's New Initiatives Group, a leading brain trust for community colleges.

Closer to home, board members from my own Northeast Texas Consortium of Colleges and Universities, including community college presidents Pamela Anglin, James Henry Russell, Greg Powell, Brenda Kays, Mike Metke, Brad Johnson, and Jerry King, are always encouraging new ways of approaching college technology and networking challenges, pushing me to think in new ways.

With the consortium based at the University of Texas Health Science Center at Tyler, I must commend those who have supported our work there and look for ways to expand our mission into the region. Of course, I will miss many but must reference Kirk Calhoun, Pierre Neuenschwander, Jeffrey Levin, Carol Davis, Mitzi Harris, John Yoder, Kris Kavasch, and Joseph Woelkers.

My own team at the consortium is unsurpassed and has provided the support and ideas that make our creativity possible. Cindy Smith, Darlene Flournoy, Irene Johnson, and Patricia Maddox provide insights and inspiration in so many endeavors. The networking group, including David Nichols, Tracy Roberts, Gordon Martin, and Jim Albright, have spent nights, weekends, and Christmas holidays facing the issues that served as a background to a number of the coming chapters.

On the home front, thank you to my wife, Janet, and to our newlyweds, Sara and Matthew, for keeping me on track and forgoing many of our weekends over the past year. Also, my thanks go to my good friends Benny Yazdanpanahi and Jay Olson, both IT specialists, for always lending an ear over a cup of tea or something a little stronger and to Geoff and Patti Willbanks for Sunday lunch discussions at Margarita's. And finally, a thank-you to my neighbors George and Joyce Singleton, who are always ready for *Dancing with the Stars* with a hot pot of coffee for Janet and me.

Mickey Slimp

Introduction

WHAT IS A THING?

So what is a thing? An inanimate object? Something without life, thought, or the ability to act on its own? In approaching the concept of an "Internet of Things" the definition of *things* is challenged.

Like the objects commanded by a sorcerer's waving wand, the tools and technology that surround mankind are suddenly moving, performing without the appearance of direct human interaction. Or when human actions are involved, they occur almost without thought.

The motion of simply entering a room or uttering a short word or phrase can kick a device or an action into motion. Preset codes and payment plans can place a car and driver at your disposal. And by the time you read this, there's a chance a robotic car will eliminate the need for the driver. Industrial chips injected into your hand might now open doors or buy a Coke in a vending machine. It seems that the inanimate objects around us have nearly taken on a life of their own.

Guided by codes and logic put into place by their designers—who themselves are sometimes machines—a multitude of "things" now react to human wishes and needs, stimulated via a connection to the World Wide Web.

As an educator and, more importantly, for students, what does this mean? Science, engineering, and health have made giant strides in just the last three or four years, all due to the automation, preprogrammed responses, sensory capability, and artificial intelligence represented by the Internet of Things.

Schools and classrooms are next.

It can be argued that anything that can be impacted by external forces, and can be programmed to adjust as a response, is or will be targeted for inclusion in the new Internet of Things. As with earlier transformations, educators will upgrade and adapt this variety of tools within a familiar teaching construct, encouraging improved and more immediate interactions with and assessments of students.

However, revolutions are rarely created and controlled by the forces of the current establishment. So the structural change that's now occurring and heralded by the Internet of Things will be generated by the students themselves, by leading faculty, and by new organizational entities most likely beyond the boundaries of the institution itself.

In the chapters to come, you will discover areas related to the Internet of Things to consider and guidelines as you plan curriculum, human resources, and facility management.

The world of the Internet of Things moves quickly. Some of the devices referenced in the coming chapters may be out of date or replaced by newer technologies even before the book goes to press. For your reading, that does not matter. The major concepts to follow will remain consistent for the coming decade, although the particulars will constantly change.

So hold on to your desk. Although it is not yet time to have a flying car in your garage (soon to be another outdated 20th-century concept), the infrastructure for driverless and even flying cars is in the works.

Fueled by IoT (an acronym for the Internet of Things), monitoring devices and internal biotechnology tools are in the works to expand the anticipated life span of today's millennials into their 100s. And during their 100-plus years, they will embark on many careers, self-reinventions, and returns to education. Part of what they will study for likely does not exist today. Other things they will need are as old as the humanities and the ancient philosophers.

It is all a part of the Internet of Things.

Chapter One

Life in the 2030s

Johnny was almost late for class. With his morning virtual study group meeting at 7:45, he had hoped for extra sleep time. But he overdid it again. The shower and getting ready had to wait.

"Study time—virtuoso," he announced to no one in particular. As his wall lit up with images of his classmates, he flopped into a comfy chair that sensed his weight, body temperature, mass, hydration factor, and mood. He opened with a "good morning, everyone."

"Hi, Johnny," smirked Cora. "I see you're not quite yourself today."

More amused than annoyed, he replied, "Thanks, Cora. Glad you noticed." He smiled at Cora's comment, happy she paid that much attention. Johnny's virtual image worked well enough to stand in for him with friends who were not as alert, but there were still quirks to real-time virtualization. The programing behind face tics and other subtle reactions was not beyond detection if you looked closely.

The "study time" command brought up his notes for the session along with an update on his assignments. He waved his hand to the right and the wall displayed a bar chart with progress for the other team members.

His coffee was already primed for him, just the way he liked it, including the supplements and vitamins his blood scan and health monitor had recommended during his final moments of rest. Food could wait until after study time and a shower. It was still two and a half hours before his on-site activities at the college and a little over two hours before the shared electric car pod picked him up.

He thought a minute, recalling the stories he heard from his mom and dad about having to drive their own cars. A vague memory from his early childhood haunted his mind. The sim-player with Roaring Twenties Gang Chase *and* Get Grandma Home, *late 20th-century traffic jam simulations, gave him a virtual sense of that time in history. No way he would want to do that for real.*

His friend Jaxon's family still had an unconverted old-fashioned garage with a mixed electric/petrol-fueled truck in it. He could recall when his family converted their empty garage to a room shared by Mom and Dad for their home workspace and sim room.

He did have his own collection, though, and still held on to the first Amazon Dot® Mom put in his room when he was just seven. He lit it up every now and then just to talk to his old friend and part-time caretaker. "Hello, Alexa," he would start. "Have you heard a new joke lately?"

"Knock, knock," she replied, and continuing to answer herself, "who's there?"

"Figs."

"Figs who."

"Figs the doorbell, it's broken."

Johnny was not sure about that one. He would ask his mom later about a doorbell. Why would anyone need a bell on a door when the house announced approaching visitors by name through facial recognition and then displayed their image on the wall?

A BRIEF HISTORY OF THE FUTURE

First coined in 1999, the phrase *Internet of Things* emerged in a presentation by Kevin Ashton to a Proctor & Gamble (P&G) corporate audience.[1] The presentation linked radio-frequency identification (RFID) to P&G's supply chain, incorporating the then red-hot Internet as a means of collecting and transporting information as data.

At the turn of the century, most computer-stored data were still entered by people, either by keying it in, pressing a button, taking a picture, or scanning a barcode. Facing time constraints (*I need to do this before my shift ends.*), short attention spans (*Is it almost time for my break?*), and inconsistent accuracy, people simply were not good at capturing data about things in the real world.

Ashton wondered why a local retailer consistently ran out of an in-demand product while the manufacturer's warehouse stored an ample supply. He argued that humans are physical, and so is their environment. Ideas and information are not the basis for society, economy, or survival. The material world is based on things. As yesterday's computers were designed for data originated by people, however, computers knew more about ideas than things. By automating data capture, he proposed, computers could gain knowledge about things.

Radio-frequency identification, or RFID, is just one of many technologies used to help machines identify objects. An umbrella of automatic data capture

Figure 1.1. Via barcodes and embedded chips, RFID technology tracks a student's activities, shopping habits, locations, medical records, and much more. ***Courtesy of Mickey Slimp***

options involving or evolving from RIFD includes bar codes, smart cards, voice and facial recognition, biometric technologies such as eye scans or fingerprints, and optical character recognition. By using RFID and these other sensory inputs, computers can observe, identify, and understand the world, eliminating the limitations of data entered by hand.

Empowering computers with the internal tools for information gathering means they can now hear, see, and smell the world in all its glory. RFID technology offered an initial route for machines to gain this first level of sensory awareness.

With the advent of wireless sensor network technologies, RFID tags, and embedded sensor/actuator nodes, the Internet of Things stepped out of its infancy and transformed personal futures and the future of the educational enterprise through a fully integrated, sensory-aware Internet.

PERSONAL TECHNOLOGY AVAILABLE NOW

The Internet of Things (IoT) is no longer a new idea. Within the last decade, Internet-connected technologies have been integrated into society in ways already taken for granted. Few now travel without using GPS technology loaded onto a phone or tablet or built into the dash of a vehicle.

Interactive voice technology like Apple's Siri, Microsoft's Cortana, or Amazon's Alexa no longer seem revolutionary. Voice-to-text is common and often works well enough that drivers forget that they still need to avoid texting. Television remotes now accept voice commands, pulling up paid services with far fewer complications, and smart televisions will speak with you directly, eliminating the remote and replacing it with a smartphone.

Smartwatches have become commonplace. Apple and Google both produce a watch that puts Dick Tracy's wristband to shame.

Here is a look at a few products that demonstrate how advanced the Internet of Things has become. See if you can connect each device's description with its name.

Table 1.1. Match the Device

Device	*Name*
1. Amazing Internet-connected glasses that contain a camera, microphone, display	a. Delphi Connect
2. Wi-Fi-enabled scales that recognize you, send your weight and body fat percentage to your phone	b. Google Glass
3. Connecting your car to your phone, allowing remote controls and diagnostics	c. HAPIfork
4. Monitor your luggage on air travel and receive a text when it arrives and how far it is from the luggage belt	d. Jawbone Up
5. Smart, wearable device that syncs with your phone and monitors your activities, calories, and sleep	e. Kensington Proximo
6. Wi-Fi-connected doorbell that allows you to remotely answer your door and receive alerts in the form of pictures to see who is there	f. LIFX
7. Wi-Fi-enabled light bulb that you can control from your smartphone	g. Nest Thermostat
8. Ice cubes pulse to the beat of the music and monitor how much and how fast you are drinking	h. SkyBell
9. Disposable diapers with built-in sensors that parents and pediatricians can use to track a child's health	i. Smart Diapers
10. Software that determines the best time to send you notifications based on an understanding of how you use your devices	j. Smart Ice Cubes
11. Sends an alert to your key fob when you move a certain distance from your phone	k. Smart Notifications
12. Learns your schedule and automatically adjusts home temperature; controllable from your smartphone	l. SmartThings
13. Electronic fork that help you monitor and track your eating habits	m. TrakDot
14. Software allowing you to control all your Internet of Things gadgets from one place—great if you are investing in all the things on this list	n. Withings Scale

Key: 1: b; 2: n; 3: a; 4: m; 5: d; 6: h; 7: f; 8: j; 9: i; 10: k; 11: e; 12: g; 13: c; 14: l

There are many devices that are not on this list—thermostats, for example. Almost every thermostat manufacturer now has a Wi-Fi-enabled smart thermostat for your home, and smart thermostats are common in corporate environments. Garage door openers can now be controlled remotely from your dashboard, phone, or tablet. Home-monitoring cameras can be accessed remotely with a phone app, including the ability to zoom, scan, and even monitor sounds.

Biosensors built into many devices allow logins via facial recognition, a fingerprint, or a retinal scan. Picture-editing programs preloaded onto many devices include facial recognition. Once a face is tagged to a photo, that face is automatically recognized in your other shots.

Website marketing is customized based on your online purchasing history or your inspection of products on various websites. Grocery stores print custom coupons based on your past purchasing habits. Your driving records and vehicle records are available electronically to state licensing agencies, eliminating the need for paper forms. Toll booths are becoming a thing of the past, and toll tags keep a record of your driving habits.

Imagine what the future will hold.

Figure 1.2. Toll booths have moved to the point of extinction in much of the world as RFID technologies, facial recognition software, and photosensors communicate with drivers' records to automate billing for highway travel. ***Courtesy of Mickey Slimp***

A DAY IN 2030

A lot of people are imagining what the future will hold. Auto shows feature a future where robotic cars move without steering wheels. Children will not grow up and learn to drive and, not totally unrelated, will plan on living healthy lives well past 100.

By 2030, a smart home will manage most household events. Lights can be programmed to automatically dim during a movie or light up based on occupants' movements. Many home events will be guided by energy consumption, as high-energy tasks coincide with power availability at lower costs—perhaps occurring after sleep in a grid-connected home or in the heat of the afternoon for someone living in a solar-powered trailer park.

As video display costs continue to plummet, 20th-century TVs and computer monitors have fused into cardboard-thin rubber- and plexiglass-like materials that can be incorporated into smart walls. Absent the restrictions on size, walls can become giant sketchpads or markerboards tied into a world of data, audio, or video resources. IoT technology is also transforming the walls to control your household security system, providing real-scale and live images of visitors at the front door or the routes and locations of deliveries on the way to your home.

The technology is in place to connect you to a personal virtual assistant as a three-dimensional hologram hovering in place or staying with you as you move. Constantly increasing in its usefulness through artificial intelligence learning algorithms and sensors, your personalized guide (or "nanny" as far as some are concerned) can assist you in every variety of your daily home tasks.

Wellness monitoring will move well beyond today's FitBit. Home devices will track personal and real-time data to report on nutrition, wellness, and health. People should be able to live longer and better. Undetectable blood sampling will identify issues at the earliest stage, gauge your diet and exercise needs, and have an automated capacity to apply beneficial treatments as needed. Improved monitoring will allow new parents to move more freely around the home, and the elderly will maintain their mobility while remaining able to stay in their homes significantly longer.

The director at the University of Southern California's Information Sciences Institute, Joe Touch, in describing the scenario of the future, wrote that the Internet has moved past being "the place hosting cat videos" to become "a seamless part of everyday life." A conscious effort of "looking on the Internet for something will be passé," said Touch, noting that "users will simply be online, and just look."[2]

Hal Varian, chief economist for Google, considered the impact that "universal access to all human knowledge" is having upon society as mobile devices and educational tools become available worldwide. "The smartest person in the world," posed Varian, "could well be stuck behind a plow in India or China."[3] As Internet devices proliferate, access to information and expanded literacy will change life and learning in so many ways.

The number of people currently accessing the web across the globe is now past 4 billion and is growing steadily, even faster than the growth in population. In her article "The Future of the Internet of Things Is Amazing, If We Don't Muck It Up," marketing professional Alisa Valudes Whyte, CEO of the Merritt Group, estimated that 4.9 billion sensors currently had an Internet connection and predicted the number to reach 38 to 50 billion by 2021.[4] The sensors, of course, are living within other machines, connected to the Internet and sharing and communicating, both with humans and with other machines. Connected cars, connected logistics, connected clothing, connected everything—they are either coming or they are already here.

So as an educator, how will all of this affect you? How will it impact the classroom, and will classrooms even be needed? What does it mean for college and other school facilities? Of most importance, how will it affect Johnny, the proverbial student of the 2030s who is entering his earliest years of schooling now?

Market leader GE Digital estimates that business-to-business applications of the Internet of Things, also known as the Industrial Internet, will potentially add $15 trillion to the global economy by 2035.[5] How much of that impact will involve education? As for the teaching profession, what changes will be forced upon faculty, or can they take the reins to guide the change?

The potential for the Internet of Things is enormous. It also presents challenges. Hackers are already turning their attention to Internet devices, from automated voting machines to the defense mechanisms safeguarding homes, business systems, and even nations. Student and personnel records are at risk, with identity theft as a prime target. Robotic cars, trains, and planes face potentially serious hacking perils, while more traditional pranksters hijack a thermostat to heat up a class or a WeMo light control to send Morse code via a dorm hallway.

SO HOLD ON. HERE'S WHAT'S COMING

Before moving on to the added challenges of flying cars, here is what will happen in the following chapters to prepare you for the flight.

You will gain a big picture of what is going on in the Internet of Things, including how devices work and interconnect, what types of devices are coming into play, and how this will impact college and other students. More and more, physical things are being replaced with software. So you will also gain insights into what the transition means and how to take advantage of it to save school funds and to be more efficient. You will learn just enough about Internet standards and protocols to avoid costly errors and keep your devices working together.

Taking a look at how IoT will impact the curriculum, the focus turns to the workplace of the future. What jobs are emerging, and what working fields are imperiled? How will teaching methods change, and what will it mean as students take more and more responsibility for their learning?

The need for security is going to be a continuing concern. In the final chapters, you will find out where the most common and the more challenging threats lie. You will learn how to "staff up" to meet the threats and other steps to keep you from harm's way. There are pitfalls out there, so it is best to be a part of the discussion, sharing ideas on how to best avoid them.

Throughout, you will get to keep your eye on Johnny and his fellow students as they explore the world of the 2030s and the grand potential and perils that are there. So hold on.

NOTES

1. Gabbai, Arik. 2015. "Kevin Ashton Describes the Internet of Things." *Smithsonian* magazine, January 2015. Retrieved from http://www.smithsonianmag.com/innovation/kevin-ashton-describes-theinternet-of-things-180953749.
2. Anderson, Janna, and Lee Rainie. 2014. *Digital Life in 2025*. Pew Research Center report, March 11, 2014. Retrieved from http://www.pewinternet.org/2014/03/11/digital-life-in-2025/.
3. Anderson and Rainie 2014.
4. White, Alyssa Valudes. 2016. "The Future of the Internet of Things Is Amazing, If We Don't Muck It Up." *Huffington Post Blog*, November 25, 2016. Retrieved from http://www.huffingtonpost.com/alisa-valudes-whyte-/the-internet-ofthings-future_b_8640360.html.
5. White 2016.

Chapter Two

The Internet of Things

After class, Johnny shrugs on his jacket and heads out the door. Locking up the house is unnecessary. Built-in sensors detect his absence and automatically activate the home security system. He can monitor activity via his smartband, the evolutionary successor of the smart watch that is essentially a four-inch wide, thin, rubber-like band encircling his wrist. Anyone not recognized by the house sensors triggers a recording and notifies Johnny.

His internship at Marble Worldwide Delivery is part of his community college experience. His work in loss prevention is preparing him for a career in efficiency management. As he enters the building, his presence is logged and his workstation is activated. He takes a seat at his terminal and nods to his coworker.

"What's happening today, Fred?"

His mentor eyes him. "You're here early. Got big plans for tonight?"

Johnny grins, as always, and Fred still chuckles. "Just pull the loss data and let me know what you find."

Johnny dons his headpiece and waves at the hologram before him. "Losses last twelve hours," he says aloud. Immediately displayed are damage claims for the period since midnight.

"Number," he says.

"Two hundred and twenty-seven," a soothing voice says in his head.

"Commonalities?"

"Fifty percent went through the Atlanta hub."

"Detail."

A graphic of a robotic forklift appears. "Sixty-two percent handled by this single device."

"Maintenance records?"

All maintenance on the equipment appears. "Equipment is mechanically sound. Maintenance records are up to date."

"Operators?"

A list of employees who monitored the robotic forklift appears.

"Correlate operators to the damage claims."

A list of damage claims and forklift monitors appears. "Forty-seven percent of damages occurred with a single monitor/operator," the computer voice says.

"Report to Fred," Johnny says as he clears the images and leans back from the monitor.

The future relies on sensors. Johnny's activities in the vignette above are not far-fetched science fiction but real-world possibilities already supported by existing 21st-century technology. While holographic workstations are not yet common, houses that lock themselves are becoming more so. The Internet of Things (IoT) has opened the door to a range of new possibilities.

WHAT IS THE INTERNET OF THINGS?

Kevin Ashton coined the phrase *the Internet of Things* to describe the network connecting objects in the physical world to the Internet.[1]

In a 2008 report titled "Disruptive Civil Technologies" by the National Intelligence Council, the Internet of Things refers to "the general idea of things, especially everyday objects, that are readable, recognizable, locatable, addressable, and/or controllable via the Internet—whether via RFID, wireless local network, wide-area network, or other means."[2]

Everyday objects include more than the obvious electronic devices encountered daily like phones, computers, or kitchen appliances. They also include more than complex technical products like vehicles or heavy equipment. Many of the objects controlled by the Internet of Things would previously not be thought of as electronic at all—basic items such as food, clothing, and shelter; repair materials, parts, and subassemblies; both commodities and luxury items; landmarks, boundaries, and monuments; and all the miscellany of commerce and agriculture.

And the interactions involved include not only thing-to-person (or person-to-thing) communication but thing-to-thing communication, where objects monitor their own actions, take corrective actions, and/or involve human interaction as needed.[3]

Looking at Johnny's internship experience, every movement of a targeted package is tracked. This happens today and is a vital part of any shipping service. Damage claims are logged to equipment. Again, current technology supports this.

Equipment used to handle packages? Amazon and Walmart have both implemented machine-centric warehousing, with the human operators working from observation booths. In other less automated scenarios, vehicle maintenance is a thing of the present, and malfunctions are captured by vehicle computers. Vehicle and equipment manufacturers can easily tell when problems arise and can take corrective action (known, of course, as *recalls*).

Forklift drivers? Most likely, only a limited amount of the data presented in the above vignette is currently captured. Doing so requires monitoring the individual. While facial recognition is widely available, privacy concerns have limited its use in the domestic environment. Companies and their insurers, nonetheless, will continue to push the boundaries here.

And while ID badges can certainly carry information, that information is mostly limited to entry or exit from a facility or department rather than tracking movement or connecting an operator to a particular piece of equipment. But the technology is in place to do so and, particularly in transportation, an initial level of built-in breathalyzers may be in place.

In a 2008 paper titled "The Internet of Things in an Enterprise Context," Haller, Karnouskos, and Schroth defined the Internet of Things as a setting where

> physical objects are seamlessly integrated into the information network, and where the physical objects can become active participants in business processes. Services are available to interact with these "smart objects" over the Internet, query their state and any information associated with them, taking into account security and privacy issues.[4]

A 2014 article within the Educause Learning Initiative described the Internet of Things as "a state in which vast numbers of objects are interconnected over the Internet and can collect data and transmit and receive information."[5]

Going a step further, once an item is electronically connected via the Internet or a closed internal network (known as an *intranet*), it can become a part of the Internet of Things. Whether it is a light with a simple on-or-off switch, a thermostat programmed to make a change when a specific temperature is hit, or a more complicated device requiring multiple switches, rheostatic devices, and binary instructions, it can now be controlled by individual or preprogrammed instructions.

Again, looking at the fictionalized example of Johnny's internship experience, many aspects of the company's communication occur as a machine-to-machine or as a machine-to-human interaction, not human-to-human. The connection between damaged merchandise and the forklift would likely have gone unreported by humans not wanting trouble. A protective shipping hub would likely not report issues, hoping for that end-of-year bonus for efficiency.

Concerning privacy issues, one of the biggest obstacles to incorporating the Internet of Things into the workplace is the human element. What employee is going to jump at the chance to have his or her every movement tracked by an employer?

As this tracking becomes more of the norm in everyday life, that issue will gradually fade. Ask a 30-year-old and a 15-year-old questions about personal monitoring devices and the response is as likely to be "how cool" as it is to be apprehensive. Still, in today's environment the Internet of Things is harboring big changes in approaches to employment.

GETTING TO NOW

Few of today's students remember the first "solid state" handheld calculator or that amazing invention the Sony Walkman. Listening to music while you walked or jogged? Aside from the ubiquitous transistor radio, nobody had thought of being able to control the music you listened to while being mobile.

Looking back, components of the Internet of Things were in development more than 50 years ago. Phil Howard, the author of *Pax Technica* (www.paxtechnica.org), has created an extensive timeline of events, with selected items shared below.[6] Should you want more detail, Howard's writings are well worth the investment.

1961—Two mathematicians invent the first wearable computer—a card deck–sized device used to predict where a roulette wheel would stop.
—UCLA and Stanford Research Institute shared the first permanent link of ARPANET, the earlier version of the Internet.
1962—Dr. Joseph Carl Robnett Licklider first envisioned cloud computing while pursuing the idea of an "intergalactic computer network."
1979—A British inventor/entrepreneur created the first "teleshopping" transaction, connecting a home TV set to a computer using a telephone line.
1983—Radio-frequency identification (RFID) technology, most commonly used for barcode scanning, was patented by Charles Walton.
1993—World's first webcam.
1994—World's first smartphone.
1995—Voice over Internet Protocol (VoIP) telephone software first created, allowing phone calls via the Internet.
1999—First M2M (machine-to-machine) communication protocol created, setting the stage for the Internet of Things.

2000—First geocache placement more than a decade prior to its popularization through the recreational app *Pokémon Go*.
—The first Internet-monitored refrigerator.
2002—Near-field communication (NFC) technology introduced, letting smart devices near one another establish a communications chain, enabling and then augmenting Bluetooth and other networking technologies.
2005—The first UN report on the Internet of Things.
2006—Bluetooth Smart technology introduced.
2008—The first use of the term *MOOC* to describe a "massive open online course," offering free access to educational courses and materials.
2009—First browser-based cloud application launched as Google Apps.
—Planetary Skin deployed as a satellite-based sensor platform to monitor climate change.
—First wireless, networked pacemaker placed in a patient, setting the stage for future Internet-driven devices.
2010—Open-source lion-tracking collars.
—First online tide-monitoring system.
—Using his stomach's own motion to generate power, a patient swallows the first ingestible health sensor.
2011—Phone apps developed to help detect skin cancer.
—First drone-delivery startup founded.
—Smart implants in cows track eating habits, health indicators, and movement.
—Tesco opens a virtual grocery in Korea.
—The first smart building-management system offers around the clock monitoring of HVAC systems, security, and resource usage.
2012—Digital data reached 207 zettabytes.
—The first Internet-connected T-shirt, featuring a programmable LED screen.
2013—Internet-connected devices enable remote monitoring of greenhouses, garbage cans, cigarettes, and much more.
—The first surgery conducted by a doctor wearing a Google Glass.
—The first commercially available cyborg, a roach with embedded electronics, created.
2014—New IoT-enabled medical devices include a remotely controlled contraceptive, contact lenses designed to monitor diabetic sugar levels, and the first connected toothbrush.
—Mobile-connected devices exceed the number of people on earth, including connected guns for the police, sensor-filled fitness trackers, and a do-it-yourself smart home kit.

2015—Driverless cars approved for road testing in the United Kingdom, and the first U.S. cross-country road test for self-driving cars.
—Crop-spraying drones cleared for flight.
2018—Over half of the traffic on the Internet is generated by non-PC sources. Wireless connections exceed "hard-wired" connections to the Internet, with the number of connected devices exceeding the size of the earth's total population.
2020—New applications and demonstration projects are continuing to expand, including civilian drones. Nearly 1,000 new satellites dedicated to IoT are to be launched, including widescale climate/agricultural monitoring.

And we're still just at the beginning.

HOW THE INTERNET OF THINGS WORKS

Using Johnny's internship example, how was the information he needed so readily available? Within seconds, he narrowed down the information and targeted the area where the most damage occurred.

In the world of 2015, it would have taken hours of human intervention to inspect equipment, pull maintenance records, look at employee records, pull work tickets to correspond with employees, and file reports. And that is *after* the connection was discovered between the damages and the equipment and/or employees.

As a concept, IoT can be understood as unified technology enabling a variety of Internet-connected objects to act collectively by accessing and/or generating information. Several commonalities are needed to make "things" work together in the online environment, including

- **identifiability**—it must be possible to identify and distinguish an individual object by a predefined code, attribute, or digital footprint;
- **communication**—objects must be able to interact and cooperate with one another or with other resources through the Internet;
- **sensing**—objects must be able to recognize and collect relevant data from and about their environment;
- **storage**—the object must have access to sufficient data storage to maintain a history and/or to plot future choices;
- **independence**—IoT Objects must contain "actuating" elements allowing them to act independently without requiring complete external control;
- **a user interface**—the object must have an interface for communication with its human partners, whether a cell phone app, a programmed computer

interface, or communication hardware, such as a touchscreen panel or a Google Home device.

An *intelligent product* can be understood as today's products enriched with the ability to interact with the environment in order to make decisions. High-level requirements of intelligent products are mentioned by several authors, who reflect on what the demand on autonomous products includes. McFarlane et al.[7] describe the intelligent product as "a physical and information-based representation of an item" that

- is uniquely identified;
- can communicate with its environment;
- retains or stores data about itself;
- can communicate information about its features, production requirements, and more; and
- participates in or makes decisions impacting its own behavior and destiny.

Autonomous control describes the processes of decentralized decision-making that can occur in data-centric structures that are without hierarchy. If the interacting elements possess the capability and possibility to render decisions, autonomous control can provide the flexibility to cope with the changing dynamics and complexity of a technology-based system to improve its outcomes.

With the increasingly common robotic vacuum cleaner, preprogrammed settings are automatically modified by the detection of unanticipated objects placed in a room. Upon detecting an unexpected toy or object, the vacuum-bot alters its planned path to move around the new element. More advanced machines could use radar or sonar to identify the intrusion. A less sophisticated device might simply include a soft bumper to identify the need to adjust the route. All the machines, however, are still awaiting a sufficient level of artificial intelligence to determine how to do so without terrifying the household cat.

For the car show debut of each year's new models, additions mark the move toward fully autonomous vehicles. Radar-based and camera sensors can detect oncoming threats, giving the car an ability to react independent of the driver, applying brakes or pressuring the steering wheel to the right or left. Harder tasks, such as parallel parking, can be managed by the vehicle's local programming, aided by GPS and Bluetooth connections.

In the case of Marble Worldwide Shipping, the computer system had already made many of the informational connections. It had linked the damages to the hub site where the claims were higher. It had located the equipment used to the time when most damages occurred and to the employee operating the equipment.

Essentially, the computer could have fired off a report directly to Fred, bypassing Johnny. However, Fred has enough information coming in that he needs employees like Johnny to filter what he gets. So although the autonomous control works well in delineating data and anticipating reports, people are still needed to provide higher-order thought processes like context, relevance, and applicability.

To act autonomously, software agents are used as representatives of intelligent logistic objects, thus decision-making algorithms have to be implemented within the agents.[8] For operating intelligent products in the mentioned assembly system, an algorithm based on the "product-type corridor" is used. This algorithm is developed for assembly systems that produce more than one variant of products.

The product moves along the product-type corridor during the manufacturing and assembly process. This means that there are variants to choose along the assembly process that allow the product to redecide which product variant to target.

In this example, a finite set of possibilities are presented to the assembly system. The line expects to encounter either Widget A or Widget B. Toss a set of headphones on the assembly line and the entire line comes to a halt, waiting for a human to walk over and remove the headphones from the process. At some point, the system will recognize the headphones, note the log, remove them, and move forward.

As Johnny arrived on campus for his afternoon class, there was a commotion on the quad in front of the Student Center building. As he approached, he saw a student lying flat against the ground with his knee arched up toward a group of nursing students who surrounded him.

The students were sending simultaneous photo streams of the student's bare and injured knee along with a voice narration to the school's Campus 9-1-1 app.

It turned out to be a class demonstration, so Johnny watched as the class documented the injury, interviewed the student on how it had occurred, and walked through the injury pathway and scenario. The nursing students had simulated this scenario several times and had delegated their responsibilities so that information was delivered to the app simultaneously from several of their phones and instruments.

Johnny had used the Campus 9-1-1 app himself in the past and found it quite useful. He had used it to report broken glass in a school parking lot and a loose handrail on one of the stairs in the math building. He had also received warnings through the app when there was a fight on campus. The warning came with instructions to stay away from the area and with a request to upload a video if he had been there when the fight broke out.

The app Johnny's school used is a prime example of one of the advantages of the Internet of Things. Using what is called *swarm intelligence*, IoT can take advantage of the collective information gathered by multiple sources at a level far beyond what can be accomplished in a regular fact-finding mission. Built around the concept of a swarm of bees, the thought is that in gathering information, two are better than one, three are better than two, and, of course, 462 are even better.[9]

By working through a variety of applications and connectors, the Internet of Things can pull together numerous devices, software, and people to work together in ways that were never before possible. Like the workers of an ant colony, tiny parts can suddenly come together from many sources to effectively work as one.

For example, schools and colleges are now aggregating cameras and related devices to provide eyes and security around campuses. Watching for

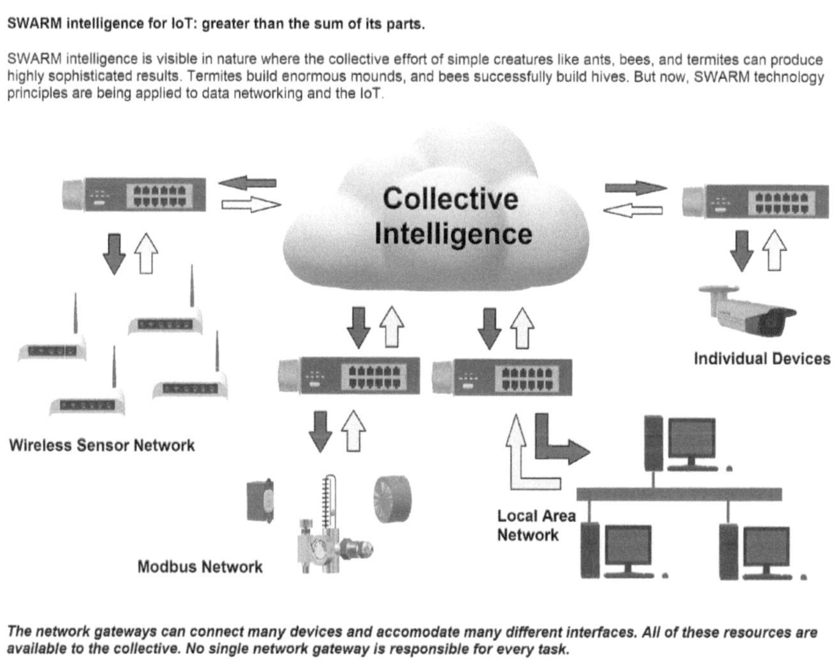

Figure 2.1. ***Used by permission from the*** **Industrial Ethernet Book** ***87, p. 12. Courtesy of Tim Taberner***[10]

physical violence, threats, or simple traffic control, they expand the capability of campus security officers to monitor a school from multiple points while remaining in their office or in their cars. Now it is only logical to expand upon the possibilities. Add a monitoring capability via the Internet so that password-protected or even public access to the cameras are available from the homes or even the handheld devices of campus administrators.

Take it one step further to add the "swarm" effect. Following a campus murder or a similar event raising concerns and safety awareness on campus, students are encouraged to place an app on their phone that, with a tap, can turn their phone into a video or voice monitor hooked directly into a call center.

Designed for events like school shootings or simple accidents, the devices can be triggered for obvious or discrete monitoring, according to the situation. Once successfully deployed, the results supply campus officers with a barrage of real-time information as an event unfolds.

STANDARDS, ROUTERS, BRIDGES, AND GATEWAYS—OH MY . . .

Now for an introductory note on the workings of IoT. The Internet of Things can only work when the devices involved can communicate with one another. This discussion will go deeper into the networking details in Chapter 6 but for now suffice it to say that the communication involves a variety of networking standards and tools known as *switches*, *routers*, *gateways*, and *bridges*.

All the tools direct information based on Internet addresses. You are familiar with web addresses, such as www.mycollege.edu or www.rowman.com, but behind every website is an Internet protocol (IP) address that appears in a format like 40.292.82.140. A college will be assigned a string of addresses by the American Registry of Internet Numbers (ARIN), which it will use for its primary network and for differentiated secondary applications or services.

The addresses are identified by switches allowing access to campus networks and routers, which direct the traffic along the network pathways to find the clearest and fastest Internet pathway between one location and another.

As the Internet traffic reaches its new location, it may have to pass through a gateway to gain entry. Gateways can involve both specific hardware and software to determine what can enter into your local area or college network.

A strong gateway can be a wonderful tool for warding off the multitudes of spam that haunt your inbox and for protecting your campus from the daily hoard of viruses and hacking attacks swimming through the open Internet. However, the gateway can also be a nuisance as a broader array of protocols come into play from the variety of devices attaching to the Internet of Things.

Figure 2.2. Student apps tying smartphones and smartwatches into the campus information and security systems can provide hundreds of eyes on a crime scene or other campus emergency. *Courtesy of the U.S. Department of Justice*

Bridges are also in play throughout the process, guiding information with standard protocols into and between networks. Information should be able to jump across protocols where the bridging technology is in place. IoT-sensitive bridges are also coming into play, built with a basic core of hardware but using a changing array of software to manage multiple protocols and a wider range of Internet addresses.

So you now have a very basic understanding of what the Internet of Things is and how it is coming into use across a variety of fields and an introduction to the technology that makes it possible. For those on your campuses who need a deeper understanding, just delve into the cited sources in the endnotes to open the door to a broad depth of knowledge.

For most readers, however, your interest lies beyond how IoT works to a focus on *how it will impact your students and schools*. You also want to know how to take advantage of the possibilities the Internet of Things opens for your college. That is where the coming chapters will lead.

NOTES

1. Claveria, Kelvin. 2017. "Meet Kevin Ashton, the Visionary Technologist Who Named the Internet of Things." Vision Critical, April 10, 2017. Retrieved from https://www.visioncritical.com/kevin-ashton-internet-of-things/.

2. National Intelligence Council. 2008. *Disruptive Civil Technologies: Six Technologies with Potential Impacts on US Interests Out to 2025*, pp. 27–31. Conference

Report CR2008-07. Washington, DC: National Intelligence Council. Retrieved from https://www.dni.gov/files/documents/2008%20Conference%20Report_Disruptive%20Civil%20Technologies.pdf.

3. National Security Telecommunications Advisory Committee. 2014. *NSTAC Report to the President on the Internet of Things*. Washington, DC: National Security Telecommunications Advisory Committee, Department of Homeland Security, November 19, 2014. Retrieved from https://www.dhs.gov/sites/default/files/publications/NSTAC%20Report%20to%20the%20President%20on%20the%20Internet%20of%20Things%20Nov%202014%20%28updat%20%20%20.pdf.

4. Haller, S., S. Karnouskos, and C. Schroth. 2009. "The Internet of Things in an Enterprise Context." In J. Domingue, D. Fensel, and P. Traverso (eds.), *Future Internet—FIS 2008: First Future Internet Symposium, FIS 2008 Vienna, Austria, September 29–30, 2008 Revised Selected Papers*. Lecture Notes in Computer Science 5468. Berlin: Springer.

5. Educause Learning Institute. 2014. "7 Things You Should Know about the Internet of Things." October 2014. Retrieved from https://library.educause.edu/~/media/files/library/2014/10/eli7113-pdf.pdf.

6. Howard, Phil. 2015. "Internet of Things Timeline." In *Pax Technica: How the Internet of Things May Set Us Free or Lock Us Up*. New Haven, CT: Yale Press. Retrieved from http://paxtechnica.org/?page_id=16.

7. McFarlane, D., S. Sarma, J. L. Chirn, C. Y. Wong, and K. Ashton. 2002. "The Intelligent Product in Manufacturing Control." Draft, submitted to *Journal of EAIA* July 2002. Retrieved from http://citeseerx.ist.psu.edu/viewdoc/download?doi=10.1.1.126.7221&rep=rep1&type=pdf.

8. Ganji, Farideh, Ernesto Morales Kluge, and Bernd Scholz-Reiter. 2012. "Bringing Agents into Application: Intelligent Products in Autonomous Logistics." Research Gate, May 7, 2012. Retrieved from https://www.researchgate.net/publication/265038206_Bringing_Agents_into_Application_Intelligent_Products_in_Autonomous_Logistics.

9. Taberner, Tim. 2018. "SWARM Intelligence for IoT: Greater Than Sum of Its Parts." *Industrial Ethernet Book* 87:12. Last updated January 5, 2018. Retrieved from http://www.iebmedia.com/index.php?id=10853&parentid=63&themeid=255&showdetail=true.

10. Photo excerpted with permission from D. Drysdale, W. Modzeleski, and A. Simons. 2010. *Campus Attacks: Targeted Violence Affecting Institutions of Higher Education*. Washington, DC: U.S. Secret Service, U.S. Department of Homeland Security; Office of Safe and Drug Free Schools, U.S. Department of Education; Federal Bureau of Investigation, U.S. Department of Justice. Retrieved from https://www.fbi.gov/stats-services/publications/campus-attacks.

Chapter Three

The Student as an Endpoint

Technology must be like oxygen: ubiquitous, necessary, and invisible.

—Chris Lehmann, Principal of Science Leadership Academy

THE UBIQUITOUS USE OF TECHNOLOGY

No matter the technology behind the Internet of Things (IoT), an educator by definition must continue to focus upon his or her students and the opportunities that technical change brings to them.

Technology's increasing capability through analytics to gauge the progress of the individual within the collective of the classroom is fascinating. Data is now constantly available on student "time on task," websites and pages on a digital text they have perused, and even their external activities.

Yet even while IoT will allow users to directly target the individual, the irony is that it occurs by establishing the student as one of the "things" in the equation. It is up to the educator, however, to ensure that the student learning remains the focus in the mix of data, always aware that the student is the endpoint for the integration of new technology.

Over the coming decade, the number of students completing associate degrees upon high school graduation should continue to increase. In some school systems, the percentage of seniors receiving associate degrees while in high school tops 90%. Pathways to two-year degrees are also broadened by "credit for life experience" programs and accelerated "competency-based" offerings.

And yet this is not enough. Particularly for students who originate in a small-town, rural environment, their isolation can leave them stranded in low-skill, minimum wage jobs or force them to abandon their hometowns looking for career opportunities. While it could be argued that "at least they are working," even the low-skill jobs in the smallest parish require a comfort with technology that is often missing.

For many rural communities, the school district remains one of the few anchors holding the community together. Often the largest employer in a small town, the school districts fiercely combat consolidation. Individually, however, many lack the resources needed to sponsor more than a few extracurricular programs, and they battle to fund any innovations in curriculum or technology.

THE RURAL DILEMMA

Throughout the United States, rural students make up approximately 24% of the total student population. At the same time, more than 55% of the school districts in the United States are classified as rural.[1] Compensation for teaching students from the most socioeconomically disadvantaged backgrounds remains low, with state funding for the same areas continuing to decline through the first two decades of the 21st century.

Poorly funded urban districts, however, are not without their own issues. Parental "flight" from diverse income level and multiethnic city schools has also diminished the educational resources and opportunities for many schools. Home, private, and charter schools likewise are not devoid of problems. The frequent closings of new nonpublic schools many times reflect the low population and critical mass issues facing rural schools.

Limited regulation of the nonpublic schools also leads to a wide range of quality outcomes, ranging from elite, Ivy League prep high schools to family-specific home schools chartered to isolate children. Stories of family-based torture in a 2018 private home school in California and a trial concluding in North Carolina the same year point to the extremes of the movement.

Both in poor urban and rural districts, the depth of the students' computer literacy may be brought into question. The poorest students may have had little more than a television or a cell phone in the home. Connectivity has been an added expense, competing with heating and "food on the table" for scarce funds.

As a result, nearly one quarter of U.S. students not only encounter difficulty receiving the background in technology desperately needed to compete for 21st-century jobs, they often miss the higher education opportunities so readily available to students in the more prosperous cities and suburban areas.

How does technology and the Internet of Things fit into this scenario? Consider Javier. His family lives in a small, rural community of about 1,500 residents located in a sparsely populated area. The closest city with a population of 100,000 is nearly two hours away. The community college serving his rural school district is 90 minutes away.

Javier's father dropped out of school so that he could help support the family. He married young. Javier is the oldest of five children and, while he is still in high school, will be the first in the family to earn a college degree.

Javier's small, rural school has done some amazing things, all involving a focus on student success. Since the turn of the century, Javier's school district has:

- implemented a research-based project focusing on student success and college completion beginning in the elementary grades;
- worked with the community college to allow high school freshmen to begin taking college-level courses online;
- provided all students in grades 9–12 with laptop computers;
- worked with a regional K–12 education service center to install wireless access points in all school buildings;
- entered into an agreement with a regional university so high school students can access university library resources online, greatly expanding the availability of materials;
- implemented high-demand career training programs in the sought-after fields of robotics, energy technology, drone applications, and health care at the high school level; and
- in cooperation with the community college, established a seamless transfer pathway to the university for completion of a four-year degree.

None of this would have been possible without the technology to support students and the programs, the Internet to provide a connection to the broader world, and the forward-thinking administrators who envision possibilities. Javier, and many students like him, will be prepared for the jobs of the future regardless of their socioeconomic status, their physical location, or their family history.

DIGITIZATION OF THE PERSON

As early as 1913, Americans were issued an identifiable number as the first driver's license laws took effect in New Jersey. In 1936, ushered in by the New Deal, social security numbers became common—at first, issued regionally. Thus, the trend of creating a digital imprint for every American citizen began.

The earliest digits (numbers) assigned to each person were accomplished without digital barcodes bars and computers. Yet they made classification of the entire population possible.

Other identifiable numbers included addresses and telephone numbers. Apart from social security numbers, however, most other identifiers could change based on the more-or-less "permanent location" of the citizen.

With the advent of number portability, telephone numbers could become a permanent part of an individual, at least as long as he or she remained within an area code. No longer did a person need to change his or her phone number with every move across town or even a few counties away.

Cellular phones took portability a step further, allowing users to be contacted no matter where they were in the country or even the world. Your cell phone number has become a part of who you are, following you everywhere and allowing anyone to contact you.

Credit/debit cards also become permanent parts of who you are. Even when dealing with a local hometown bank, the card works by being integrated into a multinational network. At a client's convenience, his or her debit card can get cash from ATMs around the world. Each card activity stamps the time, date, location, general purpose of the purchase, and the amount into a permanent digital database.

When buying tickets for international travel, customers will likely be contacted by their credit card company for verification and to inform them that the account has been flagged for approved overseas use.

Enjoy digital photography? Think about this. Almost every retail location is equipped with security cameras. Digital images of all shoppers are captured. The Department of Permitting Services takes photos for driver's licenses or other IDs. That information is all fed into databases, which, with the Internet of Things, continue to be interconnected. So it is not a stretch to realize that somewhere someone has the ability to track and retrace a person's every movement. As any fan of crime dramas is aware, with the widespread use of street cameras and facial recognition, a computer can identify anyone with relative accuracy wherever his or her image is captured.

Like the GPS mapping on your smartphone? Not only will Google Maps or similar programs keep up with where you are and direct you to where you want to go, they enable tracking and keep a record of your location. You become the latitude and longitude of your location. When combined with your unique phone number and your face, captured by a security camera, it is easy to determine where you are and what you are doing.

Smartwatch wearer? Same thing.

So *big brother is watching*, but before going all Orwellian, realize that you have agreed to this digitization of your person based on the benefits it provides. Need help? You are easy to find. Have an accident? You can be located and help is on its way.

How much is available about you by way of public information on the web? With a simple search and $29, one of the authors found out quite a bit about himself. This excerpt is compressed from about 20 pages of information. Some names and locators have been modified for privacy. For $29.00, however, you can break through the privacy concerns to find this on your own…

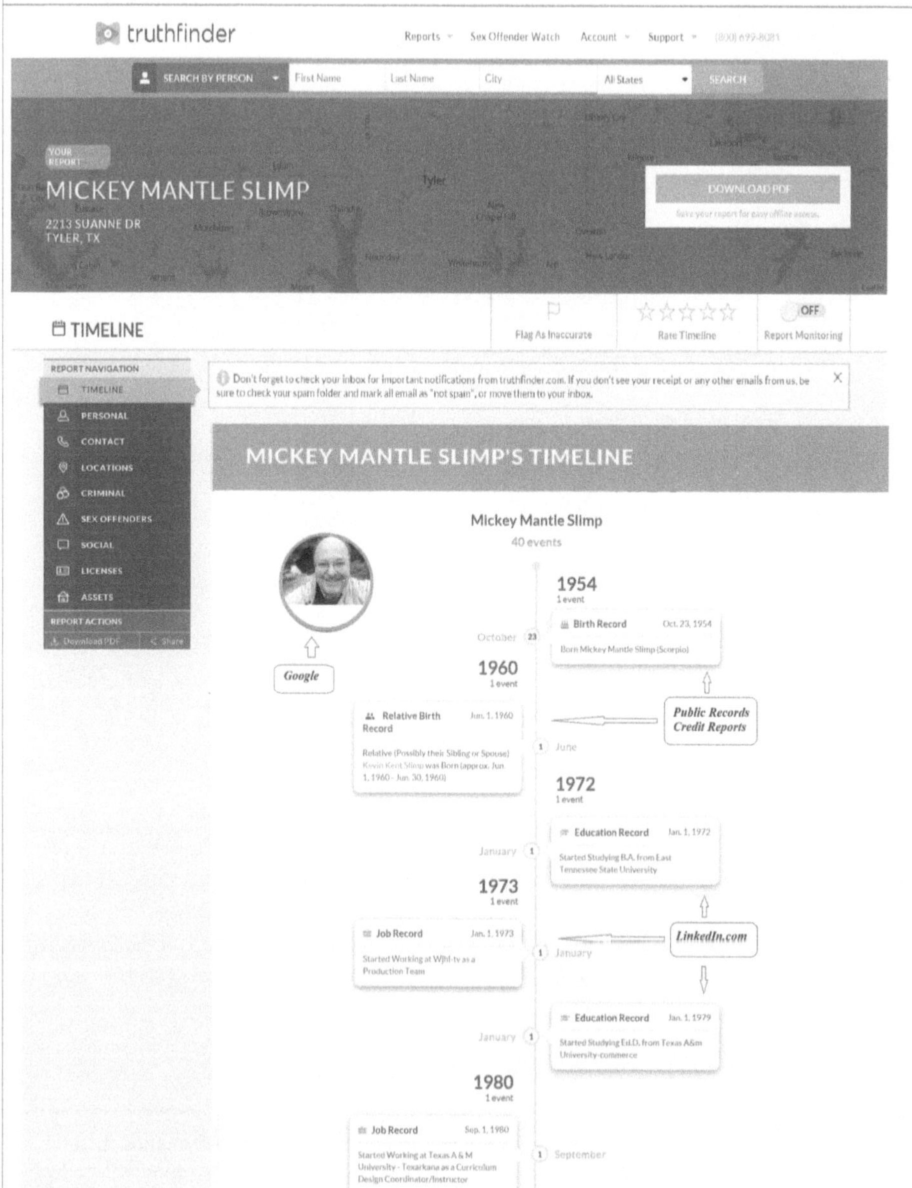

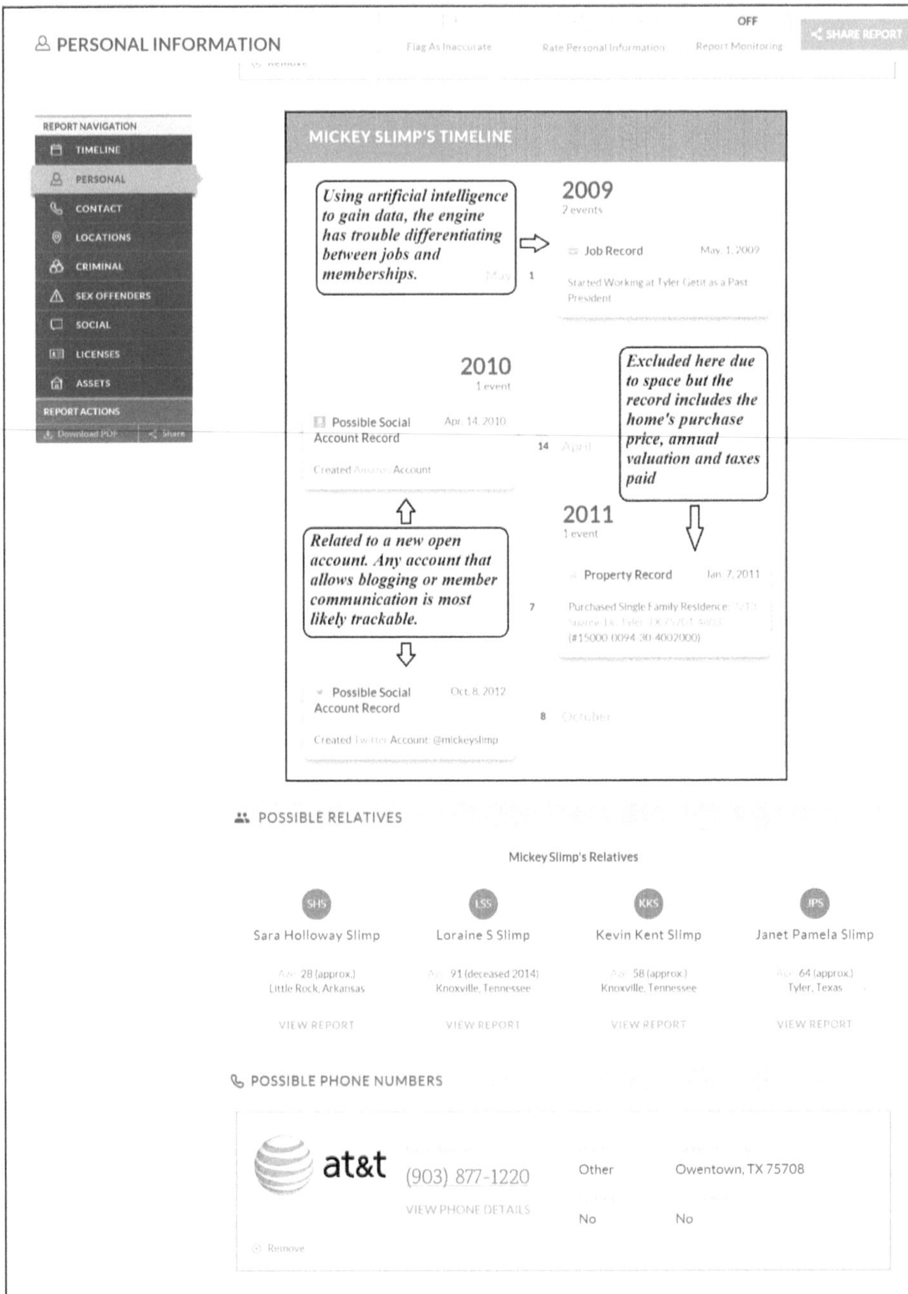

As most of the information is acquired through algorithms that pull the information directly from sites using artificial intelligence to make judgements on accuracy, the report will reflect issues common with the source sites. For example, LinkedIn may have difficulty distinguishing between a full-time position and an office in a professional association, listing both on a similar level.

Want to see who else in the bar or restaurant might be single and looking? There is an app for that and it uses your location. Want your friends to know you're standing under the Eiffel Tower? Pin it and your location appears on Facebook. Someone steal your laptop? Use an app on your smartphone to locate and disable it. Someone steal your smartphone? Same process.

You have been digitized, as have your students. There are privacy issues that will continuously be grappled with. But for educational purposes, this can be a tool for learning. That is not a completely bad thing.

THE DIGITIZATION OF PERSONAL EFFECTS

Johnny's grandparents went through their own digitization. Here is a look at how it happened.

It is 1961 and little Loretta is in the first grade. She proudly carries her book satchel, which includes her Big Chief tablet and her oversized pencil, to school. She is looking forward to learning to write like her mommy does and learning to read like her daddy.

After school, she gets to watch cartoons on TV. They just got "the cable" at their home and now have more than two channels to choose from. Daddy keeps telling her not to twist the channel knob off of the TV, but she likes turning it and that way can always find a cartoon. She even got to stand by the ladder when her daddy pulled the big antenna off the roof.

"What a modern age we live in," said her dad as he stepped off of the ladder.

Loretta cannot wait to show her cousin Lily. Lily lives in the country and they only get one channel.

Fast forward to 1972. Lily has moved to town and is in the same high school as Loretta. Lily is in Loretta's physics class and is admiring her brand-new calculator. Powered by batteries, it is small enough to fit in her purse.

"Just look at this," says Lily. "It adds subtracts, multiplies, and divides. It even does sines and square roots."

As Loretta picks it up, she thinks, So cool. I hated having to carry around a slide rule. *At the same time, she wonders how such a tiny device can do so many calculations. And it was so fast!*

After school, they study at Loretta's for their math test, checking their answers with Lily's new calculator. "I have a new cassette tape," said Loretta. "Olivia Newton-John. Can you believe they can get fifteen songs on here?"

As they study, Dad looks in from the hall. "Is that a calculator, Lily? I've been wanting to get one myself."

Lily and Loretta explain the calculator to Dad, only pausing to flip the cassette over when the music ends. Thanking the girls for the demonstration, Loretta's dad stands up to leave.

"What a modern age we live in," he says, stepping out the door.

It is the mid-1970s and Loretta and Lily soon will graduate from community college. With associate of science degrees, the world is at their feet. Lily scans the want ads. "Look, Cousin. Here's an ad for keypunch operators. Think we would enjoy that?"

Loretta comes to look at the ad. "Yes. My dad already mentioned it to me. He says it's not that different from using a calculator and that computers have a better future than even plastics."

Lily's eyes widen. "So you think we could get jobs working with computers?" she said, more a statement than a question. The next week both started work for the City of Austin.

Keypunch operators, *thought Loretta.* Wow! A job like this could last for years.

"What a modern age we live in," smiled Lily as they left the interview.

By the late-1990s, both Loretta and Lily have husbands and families, and their kids are now ready to go off to college.

As a soon-to-be empty nester, Lily has decided to try her hand at writing. Neither she nor Loretta had gone back to work after being laid off from the mainframe team. But now she is thinking of bringing her skills back to play with a home computer. She picks up her Motorola flip phone and calls Loretta.

"Want to come over for coffee?" Lily and Loretta live on the same street, so morning coffee is a common practice.

"Sure. Let me put my face on and I'll be right there."

Cell phones. Loretta thinks about how great it is to have a phone that works all over town and that is small enough to fit in your pocket. She hurries over to Lily's.

"Remember back when we worked with punch cards?" Lily asks Loretta over coffee.

Loretta chuckles. "We were two high-tech ladies, weren't we? I guess it's good we both met and married cops before our cards were punched."

Lily reaches for a color flier from the newspaper. "Look at this, Lori. An Apple iMac is only $1,299. I know they've been out for a while. But now the prices are coming down, I think this could be a good investment for my writing."

Loretta reaches for the flier. "What all can it do?"

Lily shrugs. "I'm not sure about it all, but with a modem you can send and receive electronic mail. There's a new service called America Online that costs about ten dollars a month and lets you mail others, read the news, and even shop from your home. A lot of people on AOL are putting up what they're calling websites to share information."

"Well," says Loretta. "Why don't we get grab lunch somewhere, then go to the store this afternoon and find out more about it."

As they walk out the door, Loretta shakes her head while thinking about a computer being small enough to fit in a home. She smiles as she hands the paper back to Lily. "What a modern world we live in."

It is 2009. Loretta texts Lily from her Blackberry. "Did you see the pictures of my grandson Johnny on Facebook?"

Lily texts back, "I haven't logged on yet. Wasn't he just born?"

Loretta: "Yes, and they are so proud. He's our cute little baby boy."

Lily: "How did they get that on the Internet?"

Loretta: "My son-in-law has an iPhone with a built-in camera."

Lily: "Coming for coffee?"

Loretta: "Sure."

Lily: "Bring your new MacBook. I want to check it out."

As she slips her MacBook Pro into her backpack, Loretta marvels at the devices they have today. It is hard to imagine that her son's new cell phone can surf the Internet and how powerful computers you can carry around have become.

It is 2017, and Loretta and Lily are lounging on the chaises on Loretta's deck. Lily is checking the news on her watch.

Loretta glances at her. "Don't you ever read a newspaper anymore?"

"Do they still have newspapers?" Lily keeps studying the news headlines on her watch.

Loretta's phone rings like a doorbell. She picks it up and studies the screen. "My Amazon delivery is here." She glances at Lily as she touches the screen. "Just go on in and leave the package inside the door."

"Yes ma'am," the Amazon delivery driver says. Loretta watches the screen while she unlocks the door from a distance. The driver sets the package inside and closes the door before leaving. Loretta locks the door.

"What did you order?" Lily asks.

"A new set of dominoes for Mexican Train. It has digital scoring."

"How does that work?"

"Each player is identified by location. The game knows where a particular domino came from based upon that location. Scores are automatically calculated based upon the value of the domino and the location of the players."

"That sounds interesting." Lily glances at her watch again. "So when are we playing?"

"Let's see if the girls are free for tomorrow night."

Lily touches her watch and asks, "Do I have any appointments tomorrow night?" The watch responds in a lifelike voice that no appointments exist. "I'm free."

Loretta sends a digital calendar invite to their gang of gals, and they sit back to enjoy the rest of their coffee. What an amazing world they live in.

STUDENT MASTERY OF THE DIGITAL ENVIRONMENT

Incoming college freshmen for fall 2018 classes were born in the 21st century. These students never knew a time when the Internet did not exist. Their lives are surrounded by instant information, instant communication, and instant entertainment. With few exceptions, they are the definition of digital literacy.

The National Council of Teachers of English defined digital literacy as the ability to[2]

- Develop proficiency and fluency with the tools of technology;
- Build intentional cross-cultural connections and relationships with others so to pose and solve problems collaboratively and strengthen independent thought;
- Design and share information for global communities to meet a variety of purposes;
- Manage, analyze, and synthesize multiple streams of simultaneous information;
- Create, critique, analyze, and evaluate multimedia texts;
- Attend to the ethical responsibilities required by these complex environments.

The American Library Association's Digital Literacy Task Force defined digital literacy as "the ability to use information and communication technologies to find, evaluate, create, and communicate information, requiring both cognitive and technical skills."[3]

Digital literacy has become one of the primary teaching goals in most schools and continues to grow as a necessary outcome of the learning process. It is also no longer an optional skill for teachers and college administrators. The days when an assistant could be relied upon for all technical support is no more.

STUDENT USE OF SOCIAL MEDIA

Digital literacy is all about the use of social media in the learning environment. So if you think social media is only about socializing, think again. A quick web search of "social media in the classroom" netted 97,800,000 hits.

Narrowing that search to scholarly articles only, the result still showed over 1 million results. Further narrowing that search to scholarly articles on social media in the classroom for the current year only limited it to 6,290 results.[4]

While social media does appear to be a popular educational instrument, the use of social media does carry a certain amount of risk. In an article on social media in the classroom, six pros and cons emerged.[5] Arguments for social media included:

1. Engaging students leads to greater success. Internet access and social media provides students with a breadth of opportunities to interact with others in ways that could never happen in a regular classroom. Engagement and exposure lead to greater creativity and motivators for success.
2. Structured and supervised social media usage "teaches important life lessons." By using social media under the guidance of faculty, students can see the benefits and pitfalls of the platforms, learning how to use them appropriately.
3. Collaboration beats "cliquish behavior." Students feel freer to share their thoughts "in a less personal setting" and are likely to interact with students they would not approach in a classroom.

On the other side, the arguments stated:

1. The web is primed for cyberbullying. Teachers should familiarize themselves with risks and look for warning signs.
2. Social media takes a lot of time. If you have a social media account, you know how easy it is to log on to check it *quickly* and end up spending several hours.
3. The web can be a dangerous place. The Internet is loaded with violent and pornographic images and language. Teaching students to be aware of and to avoid the dangers is a must when encouraging its use in class. By college age, most students are aware of and have mastered this. The involvement of underage dual credit students on many campuses, however, requires special caution.

THE 21ST-CENTURY STUDENT

For any campus with student housing, one of the primary complaints is not enough bandwidth to meet student demand. The complaint comes in a variety of forms, but the student expectation is always alive. Today's student does not believe she or he should have to ask for enough Wi-Fi to do whatever he or she wants. Students simply expect it to be there.

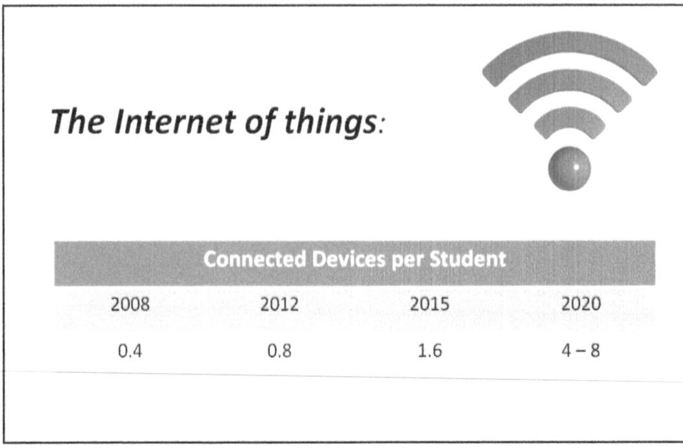

Figure 3.3. The number of devices per student has and will continue to grow as a result of the Internet of Things. ***Courtesy of Mickey Slimp and Roy Bartels***

In an environment where the primary objective should be education, most chief technology officers will agree that the highest bandwidth usage comes from Netflix, followed closely by online gaming and social media. While it could be argued that a History of the Theater course requires students to watch a movie, most students are seeking relaxation and entertainment.

Gen Z, iGen, or centennials are traditionally thought of as those born in 1996 or later. This generation defines how technology will impact future generations. The difference in thinking between Gen Z and "older" generations (including millennials) is striking. Here are some interesting examples:[6]

- Gen Z students quadruple the rate of any other generation to say that 13 is the right age for a student's first cell phone.
- Gen Zers believe phone usage at almost any time is universally acceptable—during meals, at worship, while dating, on a job or a loan interview, or even during his or her own marriage.
- Gen Z is less concerned about privacy and security when paying online with a credit or debit card than when using a mobile payment app on their phone.
- Eighty-five percent of Gen Zers—more than any other generation—are willing to trust web-based service companies like Uber and Lyft.

In a paper on "Teaching Generation Z at the University of Hawai'i," fast-paced multimedia technology was shown to impact learning in several ways:

1. A noticeable difference in the shortened attention span of Gen Z learners due to exposure to a constant stream of short segments of information and clips of no more than six seconds.
2. The use of multimedia devices resulted in an increased development of the visual ability portion of the cognitive functions.
3. Easy access to information created an expectation of instant results and constant feedback.[7]

Now take a look at Johnny and his classmate just as their morning class is winding down. Even though they are logged in remotely, the two are texting back and forth.

Johnny: Teach is v cray cray Hate read
Susan: Totes. Sub?
Johnny: Probs 15

Did you get all that? The exchange makes perfect sense to a Gen Z student. Now look at it in Standard American boomer English (SABE):

John Sr.: This teacher is very crazy. I hate reading this boring textbook material.
Miss Susie: I totally agree. Are you going to the Student Union building?
John Sr.: Probably. I'll meet you there in 15 minutes.

Why mess around with complete sentences, punctuation, and whole words when communication is easier and faster with "slanguage"? And this is a generation that frowns on email. That is "so 2012" (or to a Gen Zer, probably an eye-roll emoticon or giffy).

An emerging realization is that the education system may be failing today's learners. On several fundamental levels, the student approach to receiving knowledge differs from the way schools are presenting that knowledge. Generation Z students expect to be engaged, collaborative learners participating in their own education. Lectures and homework, pop quizzes and major tests, and working alone no longer work. Relevance, applicability, and brevity are keys to keeping the Gen Zer interested and engaged.

Another emerging problem seems to be a sort of illiteracy among the Z generation. Their email messages are often very brief and can be included within the subject line only. They rely on texting, tweeting, short Facebook posts, Instagram, and whatever other fad social networking tool is available. While Gen Zers are among the most educated students in history, their communications styles cross multiple learning channels and command visual forms of communication.

THE STUDENT IN A "MULTIVERSE"

The concept of a "multiverse" may be familiar to physics majors or comic book fans, but it is not an idea that is used day to day. As an individual, you inhabit a universe where common rules of physics apply. You understand gravity, motion, and the requirements for sustenance and well-being. But, you think, things could be better.

Since you have a time machine, you decide that it is time that you go back to 1934 and kill Hitler. You take a few tools from the 21st century with you and arm yourself with stealth technology, night vision, lidar, and whatever else may help. So outside of your personal ethical issues, your goal is relatively easy to accomplish, and you return to the 21st century.

What do you return to? A paradisal society that never suffered through World War II and developed a mixed capital-based socialism for the common good? A culture that never emerged from the global depression? Or a history where Himmler or Stalin took the reins from an assassinated Hitler and the thrust of progress remained the same, with only the villain at the top altered?

Or would you be able to return at all? Would altering history change the need for your excursion, halting it at the moment of its success? Would your personal history have disappeared, as your direct ancestors never engaged in the war, never met, and lived lives that never resulted in your grandparents or great-grandparents?

Or did you generate an alternative timeline where the history of your universe exists parallel to the history of the newly generated timeline—in essence, creating a parallel universe?

The potential for the existence of this second universe is known in the physics of time travel as a "multiverse." And an additional multiverse could be created any time the time traveler did anything to alter a past event. From H. G. Wells to Marty and Doc and to today's SyFy Network, it is a standard formula.

The Internet of Things provides students with the opportunity to learn within a multiverse. Through simulation technologies, gaming, and virtual and augmented reality, tomorrow's learner will have access to both familiar and totally foreign environments, providing a safe laboratory for experimentation and exploration.

In both the military and in the field of medicine, simulations have allowed learners entry into alternative universes for exploration and practice going on two decades. Military investments into virtual warfare simulations have morphed into home gaming consoles, which, in turn, include subtle and less-than-subtle recruitment promos for the armed services.

Medical simulations have also benefited from both military investments and National Institutes of Health support to advance the use of simulations for training and practice. Simulations developed at Texas A&M University–Corpus Christi and the Department of the Navy moved major portions of a combat medic's training into a virtual universe.

Corpus Christi's commercial partner in the project, Breakaway, Ltd.,[8] has been active in creating virtual universes for military and police training, dental practice, science experiments, and industrial training. The safety benefits of practicing with "serious games" prior to entering a real scenario is obvious. Handling hazardous chemical spills or treating a patient with a blood or airborne pathogen is far less complex after initial practice in a virtual environment.

Flight and driving simulators have offered alternative realities for training for some time but have become ever more affordable and realistic with the deployment of 3-D virtual headsets. Similar simulations will continue to expand for our students, providing submersion experiences in geography, language, history, and more.

Landlocked students have an option to conduct virtual visits through a multitude of national parks, guided by tools from the National Park Service.[9] Most parks now have a virtual component, accessible to students anywhere they can access the Internet.

Yet resources standing alone can only accomplish so much for the student. The teacher remains essential for guiding the students to and through the learning objects. Teachers also must move the students from their disjointed variety of experiences to develop meaning and assimilate their newfound knowledge, skills, and emotions. This is discussed in the next chapter.

NOTES

1. National Center for Education Statistics, Institute of Education Sciences, U.S. Department of Education. 2013. "The Status of Rural Education." Retrieved from https://nces.ed.gov/programs/coe/indicator_tla.asp.
2. National Council of Teachers of English. 2013. "The NCTE Definition of 21st Century Literacies." Position Statements, February 28, 2013. Retrieved from http://www2.ncte.org/statement/21stcentdefinition/.
3. American Library Association. 2013. *Digital Literacy, Libraries, and Public Policy. Report of the Office for Information Technology Policy's Digital Literacy Task Force*. *District Dispatch* (blog). Retrieved from http://www.districtdispatch.org/wp-content/uploads/2013/01/2012_OITP_digilitreport_1_22_13.pdf.
4. Searches performed using Google and the Chrome browser on a Mac.
5. Hosler, Aimee. 2017. "6 Pros and Cons of Social Media in the Classroom." TeachThought. Updated October 31, 2017. Retrieved from https://www.teachthought.com/technology/6-pros-cons-social-media-classroom/.

6. Center for Generational Kinetics. 2016. "Gen Z Technology Usage and Trends Infographic: The Generation after Millennials Will Change How You Use Technology." Retrieved from http://genhq.com/igen-genz-technology-trends-infographic/.

7. Dudoit, Kelley, Shirl Fujihara, Mariana Gerschenson, Ann Kennedy, Brad Koanui, Veronica Ogata, and Jeff Stearns. N.d. "Teaching Generation Z at the University of Hawai'i." President's Emerging Leader Program, University of Hawai'i. Retrieved from https://www.hawaii.edu/ovppp/Leaders/files/2015-2016-Projects/PELP_GenZ_PaperV.6.0-5.4.16.pdf.

8. Whatley, Douglas, and Walter Cheek. 2013–2018. BreakAway Games company website and author discussions. Retrieved from http://www.breakawaygames.com.

9. National Park Service. 2018. "Teachers." Retrieved from http://www.nps.gov/teachers.index.htm.

Chapter Four

Teaching in the Empowered Classroom

Progressive colleges are recognizing that the rigid, one-size-fits-all approach that has been the tradition in education for a century needs a revision, if not a total transformation. Dismay with the learning process has brought into question many of the 19th-century structures of K–12 and higher education. At the end of their journey, are graduating students ready to approach life in the 21st century, prepared both for a career and to be engaged in their community? A more personalized, student- and learning-centered design is called for, focused on increasingly diverse students.

The K–14 approach was a step forward, recognizing that a high school diploma alone meant little. A minimum of an associate degree or a postsecondary certificate became a necessity in a work environment that demands working in teams, communicating with clients, and having the discipline to show up on time, ready to work.

Today's approach is closer to a P–20 model, taking the student to the graduate level before education is complete. Accompanying this progression is an increasing need for an almost innate sense of technology.

As the emerging Internet of Things (IoT) and digitization era unveils itself, what does it mean for the classroom? Will classroom instruction become more and more automated? Will the classroom still *exist* by 2030, or will the entire instructional process occur in a virtual scenario, with students rarely or ever approaching a campus? Good questions.

The *21st Century Classroom Report*,[1] published in 2010, found that only 8% of teachers fully integrate technology into the classroom. Sixty percent of teachers *use* some technology in their teaching (LCD projectors, interactive whiteboards, lecture-capture systems, etc.), but only 26% of students indicated technology use in the classroom was encouraged. Both teachers and students reported the use of handheld technology and social media in their private lives, but less than 12% of teachers reported use of these technologies in the classroom.

The Internet of Things is influencing the percentages. In some cases, students are even leapfrogging their professors to learn almost in spite of them. YouTube (www.youtube.com), Khan Academy (www.khanacademy.org), and Explain Everything (www.explaineverything.com) are common online destinations for students who self-tutor out of class for what they miss from their traditional lecturer.

Looking at the changing expectations of Gen Z students, recall that, as a group, they multitask with ease. They absorb information in snippets. They drive their own learning yet can work collaboratively. They prefer doing a project to reading a chapter or doing sets of predetermined problems for which they see little relevance to real life.

Engaging in what some derisively see as "poke and puke" learning—poking information in by lecture, memorizing it, then spitting it out on a test—leaves little sense of accomplishment for students except those receiving an A. Where is the preparation for a future driven by technology? Employer evaluations and life itself rarely give grades for memorization.

A report prepared for the Nellie Mae Education Foundation observed that building technology usage around performance—that is, "writing, research, and analysis—rather than simply drills and practice"—provides students with an ability to "surpass the knowledge and skills typically measured in achievement tests." The foundation's areas of competency included "problem solving, creativity, collaboration, data management and communication."[2]

While employers noted that the more essential skills were missing for many graduates, the report concluded that a newer concept—"digital literacy"—would be a basic requirement in a global society. The report continued by exploring how digital literacy changes the way that students approach learning. With greater access to course content, alternative scheduling, and learning choices, students gain options to chart their own instruction. "Instead of being passive recipients of information, students using technology become active users."

UNIVERSAL ACCESS TO INFORMATION

On November 3, 2015, the 38th session of the United Nations Educational, Scientific, and Cultural Organization (UNESCO) adopted a resolution declaring September 28 of each year as the International Day for Universal Access to Information (IDUAI). In the resolution annex, the introduction stated,

> The universal right to information is essential for societies to function democratically and for the well-being of each individual. Freedom of information or the right to information is an integral part of the fundamental right to freedom of expression. It is established as a right in Article 19 of the Universal Declaration of Human Rights of 1966, which stipulates that the fundamental right to freedom of expression encompasses the freedom "to seek, receive and impart information and ideas through any media and regardless of frontiers."[3]

While a resolution in and of itself does not guarantee that all individuals will have access, it does reinforce what we already see as an almost alarming availability of news and information as it is happening. Students today expect that information is available at any time and—almost—from anywhere.

SHARING THE POWER

Within the past generation, college instruction itself has undergone what could be called a revolutionary change. Although an educator from 1980 could conceptualize the physical experience of a 2020 classroom, it is doubtful he or she would have conceived of the expansion of online instruction, the plethora of resources for instruction, or the ready access common today to literally all of the information in the world.

Combining IoT technology with Internet-connected toys, websites, and related tools, a generation is coming of age that can get to almost anything from almost anywhere. How has that changed things?

For students of the 1990s, websites were the innovation. Everyone was creating websites—including businesses and corporations, teaching institutions, and even families. The sites were labor intense. Information was manually updated, meaning that many times it was seldom, if ever, updated. Even with "refresh dates" posted on the webpages to indicate the last time information was updated, much of the information was soon stale or irrelevant. Website owners seldom realize the amount of work involved in keeping a site current.

Today, websites serve a variety of purposes, with online shopping as one of the largest. Financial empires have emerged from eCommerce, creating the wealthiest technocratic class the world has ever seen. Want a new car? You can compare makes, models, dealerships, and pricing online. Moving? The perfect house is waiting at RealEstate.com. Need a pair of shoes? An Internet search provides 628 million results. With a "one-click order," any pair you can imagine will be dropped at your door in two days—often shipped for free.

Websites offer nearly the same access to services. Individuals control their banking and finances online, paying bills, refinancing mortgages, trading stocks, and managing retirement accounts all from their phone. Check writing is largely restricted to the electronic format, and PayPal has replaced the art of "wiring" money.

Telehealth is moving physician visits to your phone, a computer, or to a Doc in a Box kiosk at a local pharmacy. Insurers are setting up their own full-service medical operations where a patient claim immediately triggers online access to a company-assigned teledoc. The result is a diagnosis and prescription quickly delivered to you with no paperwork and without leaving your home.

Quick instructions for almost any hobby or do-it-yourself home and car repairs are online. Web tutorials are legion, offering everything from how to bake a cake to how to fly a plane. If you want to know how to do something, go online. Name your interest and you can go online for tips, tricks, and "how-tos" from hundreds of others. Want to replace your own toilet tank fill valve? The web has 433,000 results, including 134,000 with videos.

Millennials, Gen Z, and even Gen Xers and boomers have become attuned to a 60-second society. The expectation is to grab a phone, pull up a website, and find whatever is needed in less than a minute. The frustration of a slow website is a relatively new emotion, unheard of a decade or so ago.

Even before 2010, the explosion of social networking had made the use of some websites obsolete. By simplifying and sharing the power of website creation to a world of users, Facebook, Twitter, LinkedIn, and a few other early contenders gained leadership of the online world.

Once posted on a social networking site, information was immediately shared with all the site's followers. No one had to find a website to learn something. They just followed an individual/company/news feed/club/group or whatever to keep up with everything they needed to know.

The power structure of the Internet had changed, along with the expectations of the users. With earlier websites, everyone had to go somewhere to gain information. With social media, the information was pushed to the users, changing the entire dynamic.

The changes in the web and the online environment have since impacted everything. Most every industry has gone through a rethinking of their business plan to both collect and push out information, capital, and services on the web. In the field of higher education, the impact has just begun.

LEARNING MODELS FOR THE EARLY 21ST CENTURY

Artificial intelligence, the Internet of Things, and the characteristics of the millennial and Generation Z students are moving the learning experience from an "inside the building" model to a number of options for student engagement. Core to the new focus is a move from a traditionally structured classroom model based on "Carnegie Unit" credits for seating time in a room or lecture hall to the recognition of a panoply of options, centered on what works best for student learning.

Students come into the learning process with a number of capabilities and motivations, which have long been recognized through Maslow's Hierarchy of Needs.[4] According to Maslow, those with little means of support and immediate needs for survival will lack the motivation and the capability to pursue a long, meandering route through an advanced program. Much like the commuter who just wishes to reach a destination as rapidly as possible, the student is looking for a short-term option that will quickly provide some income and a minimal sense of security.

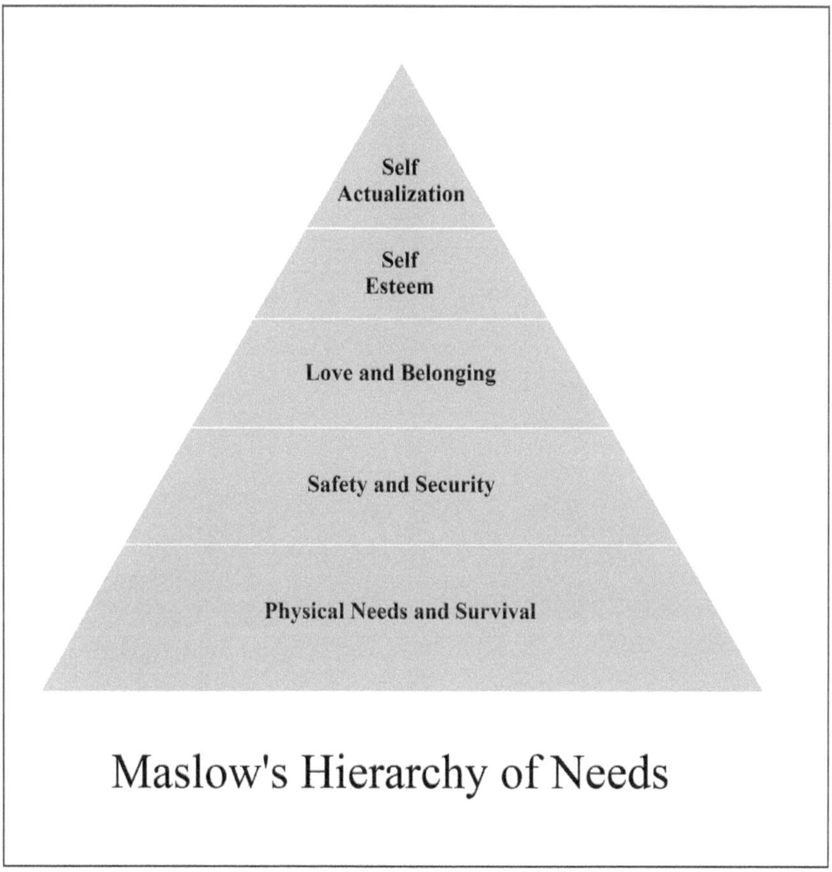

Figure 4.1. ***Courtesy of Mickey Slimp***

Competency-based instruction with a clearly defined route to completion and a flexible timeline will be a draw for students with the highest level of need or who are particularly goal oriented. As students move up on Maslow's scale, they feel safer to explore. Passing beyond the immediate crisis, they have the security to explore, seek meaning, and to self-actualize. In effect, they have more time to explore, roam, and progressively enjoy the scenery. Liberal arts, open-ended learning, and more advanced pathways become an option.

In each scenario, the Internet of Things has multiple roles to play. Consider four modes of instruction that exist today or are on the horizon.

Figure 4.2. Models for learning are changing in the classroom and beyond. Technical Innovation is allowing blended learning, with students mixing work in the classroom with work at home and other outside experiences. Learning is taking place in completely virtual settings and with augmented realities. Internet apps are allowing for *Brady Bunch* collaborations with fellow learners across a college district or with collaborative online international learners throughout the world. *Courtesy of Mickey Slimp*

CLASSROOM (TRADITIONAL) INSTRUCTION

The traditional classroom is primarily an idea of the 19th century, with the one-room schoolhouse encasing a teacher and her students. Universities used the format up to a century earlier, with professors gathering their students around them in a dedicated structure for learning.

In the industrial age, the mode took on more and more of the characteristics of the factory. Students and activities were systematized, lined up in rows, and categorized alphabetically. As the one-room model developed into a larger, multiroomed facility, students were stratified by "achievement" levels and separated or excluded based on perceived disabilities.

Just as industry fixated on clocks and concepts such as time and effort, schools did the same. Much of a student's accomplishment was measured by "seat time." Other measures of achievement depended on standardized exams that could increasingly be machine graded as the 20th century progressed.

A field trip, getting out of the classroom, was seen by students as a welcome break from the rigor of the classroom. Administratively, the event could be viewed as a frivolous distraction from book learning.

But was the classroom all that bad? The social aspects of pulling groups together into rooms, it can be argued, created a peer learning environment conducive to learning through both collaboration and competition. Resources could be maximized and shared, providing more learning options. Students had face-to-face interaction with their professors, assuring more certain observation of learning and opportunities for mentoring.

Standardization provided by a classroom environment also created the metrics that are now being used in instructional analytics. Specifically, tied to embedded Internet apps and technology, standardization provides a platform for analyzing student learning behavior. That has led to learning diagnoses and alternative strategies for improving instruction.

Within the foreseeable future, classrooms are not going away. Interestingly, the Internet of Things is one of the reasons the classroom has a future. IoT promises to expand teaching options within the classroom to access virtual field trips and resources from throughout the globe. Laboratory experiences and technology tools using virtual simulations are being integrated into classroom lesson plans without extensive setup time. And although movement is probably needed in a screen-obsessed society, the experiences are being provided as at Roane State Community College, without the requirement to schedule and move to another room or facility.

CASE STUDY: ROANE STATE COMMUNITY COLLEGE VIRTUAL HEALTH SIMULATION

By Kevin Slimp and Susan Sutton

Imagine a time in the future when students examine a live, beating human heart, floating in the air directly in front of them as they study anatomy and physiology. That time is now at Roane State Community College Center for Health Sciences in Knoxville, Tennessee.

Dr. Susan Sutton, director of the Center of Teaching Arts and Technology and Distance Education, began a pilot study in January 2017. During the spring semester, Thomas Herron, clinical coordinator, Allied Health Sciences, and David Blevins, Paramedic program director, Allied Health Sciences, began pilot testing the HoloLens in a few of their courses.

According to Microsoft, the HoloLens promises to bring hologram technology to the classroom, enabling students to visualize and work with digital content as part of "real world" experience.[a] The HoloLens looks much like an ordinary pair of sunglasses, but the built-in technology is anything but ordinary. Connecting to a Windows-based PC through a dedicated IP address, the HoloLens allows students in the classroom to see the same image as the instructor who is wearing the device.

Blevins stated, "We began using the HoloLens when teaching anatomy and physiology, and in our cardiology courses. We now are working with an application developer for hi-fidelity medical simulation to combine a static mannequin and Mixed-Use Reality (MUR) to develop an active

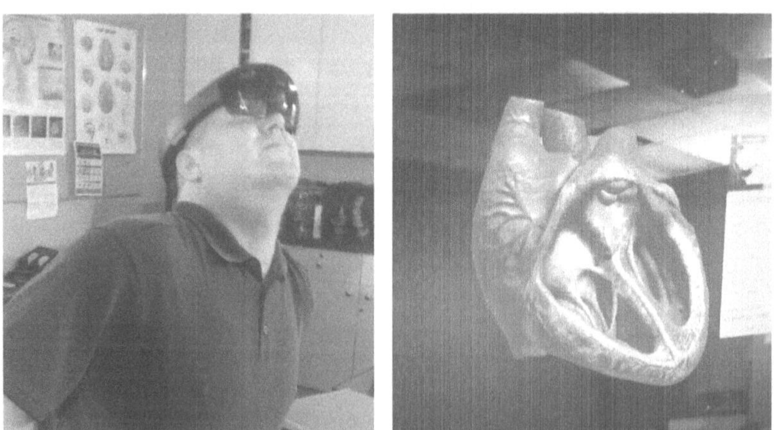

Figure 4.3. Thomas Herron teaches a paramedic class using a HoloLens to dissect a virtual heart model. ***Courtesy of Kevin Slimp***

patient with the ability to use touch senses."Mixed-use reality layers 3-D images over physical items, such as adding a virtual cardiovascular system or a muscle system over a physical skeletal structure.

While demonstrating the HoloLens, Thomas Herron explains how the technology is used to give students an up-close look at issues related to gallstones. A green line within the hologram indicates the place where hardened deposits of bile can gather in the gallbladder. These gallstones, according to Herron, "can block the bile duct and cause serious abdominal pain."

Instructors see the holograms directly in front of them. While demonstrating the HoloLens human heart application, Herron sees a beating heart as if it is directly in front of him. Students see the same image on the screen in front of the class. Using commands like "beat" and "rotate," Herron controls the image to get the view he wants. At the same time, he walks around the empty space directly in front of him. On the screen, students see a beating heart as they, too, seem to move around it. As Herron moves closer to the heart, the heart appears closer on the screen. The student sees what the instructor sees in the HoloLens.

Herron places great importance on the benefit of teaching future paramedics and EMS (emergency medical services) students using the HoloLens. "They are the ones," Herron says, "who will someday be making field diagnoses. They will be identifying heart attacks, administering treatments and beginning immediate assistance. Through use of the HoloLens," he adds, "students can learn exactly what is going on in the body when medical emergencies arise."

The Allied Health Sciences program at Roane State purchased virtual reality (VR) headsets and other apps that EMS students can use with their smartphones to see inside the body and view the activities of various organs. At Roane State, instructors primarily use the HoloLens to study the human heart and brain, although a quick glimpse into her or his own VR headset allows the student to see all the major internal working parts of the body.

Dr. Sutton explained that the Center for Teaching Arts and Technology (CTAT) created four virtual reality kits for faculty in other divisions to pilot test. The kits consist of 25 VR headsets, five iPod Touches, and a router for the classroom. The iPod Touches, which are basically smartphones without the phoning capability, allow students who do not have a personal cell with a gyroscope sensor app to participate in class.

The router places the faculty and the students on a common network, so their VR headsets can talk to each other. Within the integrated network, applications such as Google Expeditions lets the faculty member lead an

(continued)

entire group of students on an expedition within a virtual universe. Due to the expense of the technology, Sutton described the common network as "a way for CTAT to give other faculty the opportunity to give their students the VR experience."

In another area of the college, the education department teaches their pre-services teachers how to take future students on Google Expeditions. "Once the pre-services teachers are in the K–12 system," Sutton stated, "their students will have a chance to experience virtual reality technologies."

A professor in the history department uses the VR kit to take his students on virtual tours so he can show them where historical events took place. He stated that being able to see the sites in 3-D gives the students a more personal perspective of the event. In the art department, a professor uses the kit to guide students through virtual reproductions of art museums. For many, it may be their only to visit some of the famous museums throughout the world.

Administrators and faculty at Roane State believe the HoloLens is a perfect fit for younger students who grew up with digital technology.

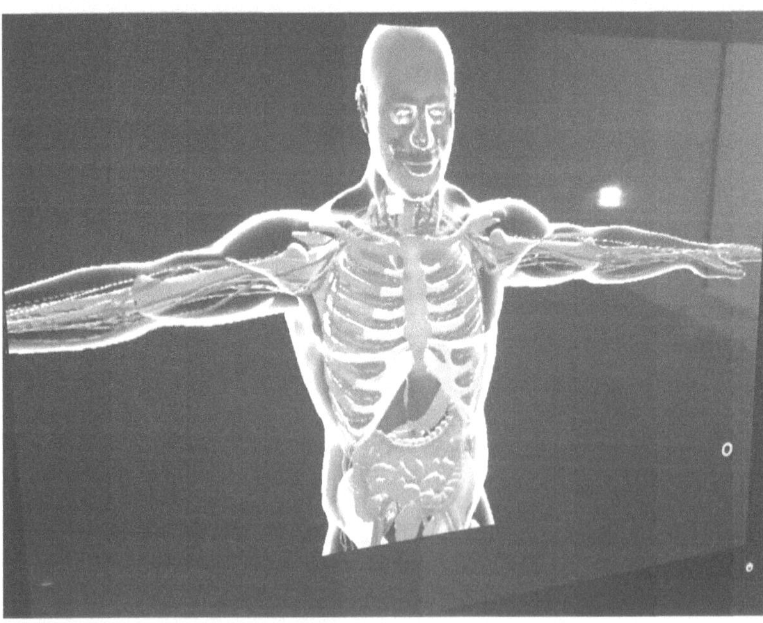

Figure 4.4. ***Courtesy of Kevin Slimp***

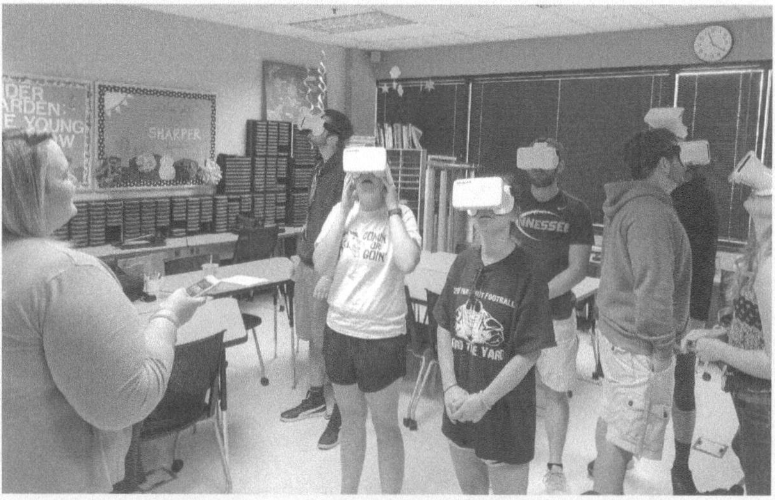

Figure 4.5. Class members at Roane State Community College explore museums and other remote sites on a virtual field trip. *Courtesy of Susan Sutton, PhD, Director of the Center of Teaching Arts & Technology & Distance Education at Roane State Community College*

If there is a negative to using the HoloLens, it is that it sometimes leads to headaches when worn for long periods due to the snug fit. Herron, however, points out, "That is usually not the case."

The HoloLens is simple to set up and use. By using an IP connection, it's much like installing any Windows-based software. Roane State purchased the HoloLens for $3,000 in 2017, with the 2018 purchase price remaining the same. A Commercial Suite, available for $5,000, included "Development Edition hardware, plus a warranty and enterprise features for added security and device management."[b] Future renditions promise to either cost less and/or offer even more innovative features.

This case study was written by Kevin Slimp, a technology writer and publisher from Knoxville, Tennessee, and Susan Sutton, PhD, the director of the Center of Teaching Arts and Technology and Distance Education at Roane State Community College.

NOTES

a. Microsoft Corporation. 2017. "Why HoloLens." Retrieved from https://www.microsoft.com/en-us/hololens/why-hololens.

b. Microsoft Corporation. 2018. "Microsoft HoloLens." Retrieved from http://www.microsoft.com/en-us/hololens/buy.

Today, classroom instruction provides a little over 60% of the educational opportunities delivered to community college students. Over the next decade, schools are likely to see those numbers decline to something like 40%. Should funding or other structures change to enable more to participate in higher education, it is likely that nonclassroom options will play an even greater role.

DISTANCE LEARNING

A formal definition of distance learning is an environment where the students are in an alternate location from the instructor for more than 50% of the time. For the most part, instruction is delivered via an electronic format—that is, through an Internet-based online learning management system, desktop video, or in classrooms connected by video.

Nonetheless, the original format for remote instruction was correspondence courses, using the mail to deliver courses via written materials and letters or written assignments between the students and the instructor. Other variations have included telecourses, delivered by broadcast, cable, or by videocassette to students, and even audio courses, which have been delivered by radio, radio satellite to remote islands, or by downloads, CD-ROMs, and various tape formats.

THE EVOLUTION OF DISTANCE EDUCATION

The beginning of this book showed Johnny attending his college class. He was not on campus. He was, in fact, at home. Now before you go and get all "college campuses are disappearing," know that colleges have been seeking remote students for decades. The 1977 formation of the American Association of Community and Junior Colleges' Task Force on the Uses of Mass Media for Learning helped solidify the presence of non-campus-based learning in America. Remote learning had been in place long before 1977.

In the mid-1840s, Sir Isaac Pitman's correspondence colleges in England took advantage of the then new free rural mail delivery to send course materials to students. In 1883, Chautauqua College in New York offered degrees to individuals who completed coursework via correspondence and who participated in summer workshops.[5]

By 1977, television took a firm hold on America, and color television sets were common in American households. Recognizing this, the Task Force on the Uses of Mass Media for Learning was interested in advancing the use of radio, newspapers, and other mass media for learning. The focus was on the telecourse (TV course) because it was the medium with which they had gained the most experience and which seemed to offer the most potential for many community colleges and large numbers of learners.

An issue of the American Association of Community and Junior Colleges' *Community and Junior College Journal* was devoted almost entirely to instructional applications of television and other media. Editor William A. Harper noted that a "convergence" of the community college and educational TV (now known as *public* or *cable-access television*) seemed only natural. Through the years, the organization changed names to the Instructional Telecommunications Consortium, and in the 1990s became the Instructional Technology Council, still an affiliated council of the American Association of Community Colleges.[6]

The concept of eLearning—that is, learning through a computer interface—developed both independently and in parallel with video and other

Schools Use TV In New Way

Mrs. Dorothie Oskar, a consultant from Lyons Carnahan, Publishers, has been teaching a group of fifth grade students in the city for the past three days how to read over television. The purposes of Mrs. Oskar's teaching: (1) to demonstrate how one teacher from a central location can enrich the instruction program of many teachers in many classrooms at the same time; (2) to show the classroom teachers some techniques of teaching reading. Many teachers have taught by lecture over television but this is the first time a teacher has taught a group of city students live over television. The programs were presented from the city school's studio at North Side School.

Figure 4.6. Early distance education using a remote teacher one day a week by cable television, with follow-up by a classroom visit by the same teacher later in the week. *Facebook site for Johnson City, Tn. Memories, posted by Ted Bowers. Original from* Johnson City Press Chronicle, Feb. 16, 1962.

technologies. Several of the earliest forms of eLearning actually transpired before any systemic work was occurring with college-level telecourses.

1960s

In 1960, the University of Illinois created a system of linked computer terminals allowing access to course materials and even recorded lectures, predating the first version of the Internet by nine years. The system evolved into PLATO (Programmed Logic for Automatic Teaching Operations). At one point, thousands of terminals around the world used PLATO. Many of the concepts of social networking prominent today can be traced to rules created with PLATO.

1970s

Recreational computer games took to education as Apple released its first popular educational offering, *Lemonade Stand.* Developed in 1973 by Bob Jamison, the game was ported to the Apple II platform by Charlie Kellner in 1979.[7] The concept was popular and generated *FaceMaker* and other games by Spinnaker Software, leading to one of the greatest games of Gen X, *Oregon Trail.*[8]

1980s

To encourage the use and expansion of online courses, the Electronic University Network offered an online course for use with Commodore 64 and DOS-based computers. Students used proprietary software and modems to interact over telephone lines. Personal computers became refined and popularized, with upgrades to the TRS-80, the Commodore 64 evolving to a graphics-based Commodore Amiga, and the Apple IIe evolving to the first Macs. In 1981, IBM jumped into the fray with the IBM PC, introducing an early version of MS-DOS.[9]

1990s

The year 1994 saw an Internet-access boom. In addition to America Online (AOL), Delphi, and CompuServe, many local Internet providers offered an outlet to the World Wide Web using personal computers in the home and office. California's CALC (Computer Assisted Learning Center) evolved into CALCampus and provided real-time online courses with interaction.

Figure 4.7. *Courtesy of Mickey Slimp and Cindy Smith*

A BRIEF HISTORY OF

DISTANCE LEARNING

THE 21ST CENTURY

2002

Sloan Foundation initiates an annual survey of college and university online studies. A decade later Sloan becomes the **Online Learning Consortium**.

The **Open Educational Resources (OER)** movement is kickstarted as M.I.T's **OpenCourseWare** project starts providing lectures and course materials online for free.

2003

CALCampus moves its first courses through the **World Wide Web (www) - Houston Community College** and other 2-year schools follow.

Linden Labs releases **Second Life**, a web-based universe that popularizes virtual environments and personal avatars.

2004

ITC, a council of the American Association of Community Colleges administers its first national survey of community college trends and best practices in online learning.

2009

The US Dept of Commerce and the FCC establishes targets for educational broadband, while initiating a $4.7 billion **Broadband Technology Opportunities Program (BTOP)**. Thousands of miles of fiber optic "information highways" constructed by 2017.

2014 - Present

Wider Internet deployment sparks an exponential growth of personal digital technologies, including smartphones, wearable devices, and imbedded applications within vehicles, appliances, building materials, medical devices, and even within the person.

Figure 4.8. *Courtesy of Mickey Slimp and Cindy Smith*

Established in 1997, California Virtual University provided information pertaining to online courses offered by California colleges and universities. The number of online resources with information about online education exploded. Before the end of the decade, a number of community college virtual initiatives had begun, including the Kentucky Virtual Campus, the Virtual College of Texas, the Michigan Community College Virtual Learning Consortium, and Colorado Community Colleges Online.

Created by the Sloan Consortium, which would later become the Online Learning Consortium (OLC), the *Journal of Asynchronous Learning Networks* (*JALN*) began. The peer-reviewed publication served as a harbinger for academic research focused on online formats for distance education.[10]

2000s

Initiating what will become known as the open educational resources (OER) movement, MIT's OpenCourseWare project gave free access to the university's course materials and recorded video lectures. Widely put to use in the Third World, MIT gained a new tool for identifying previously unrecognized talents for potential recruitment from the far corners of the globe.

Under the leadership of Fred Lokken, *Trends in eLearning,* an annual survey of attitudes and practices in community colleges, tracked the change in attitude toward distance learning. First conducted in 2004, by 2016 the study showed that a number of schools enrolled 40–60% of their students at a distance.[11] Even earlier, by 2012 most respondents recognized that online education courses matched traditional classroom courses in terms of quality and results.

ELEARNING—AN EDUCATIONAL CRUCIBLE FOR IOT

Many of the instructional changes impacted by the Internet of Things are originating from within the distance learning environment. The growth of instructional analytics, documenting student participation in a course, visits to a website, uses of library and external web materials, and the focus of an eye on a page, have emerged from the learning management system structure.

The use of biometrics, using fingerprints, eye-scans, and voice patterns to identify who is working at the other end of the network, was integrated into instruction to verify test takers for remote exams and to assure financial aid auditors that the online students were specifically completing their own assignments.

Online student support, such as remote tutoring, library services, including "embedded librarians," student information and enrollment, financial aid applications, and electronic accessibility options, have each emerged or evolved in parallel with the eLearning and distance education movement.

Students increasingly are using their phones and personal devices as the primary interface with their online courses, adding to the technology demands on their colleges. As technology-oriented faculty are drawn to teach in the "geek" environment of distance education, they are likewise apt to tackle and integrate online apps into their teaching repertoire.

The schedule[12] for eLearning18, the annual conference of the Instructional Technology Council, was informative. Session titles included

- Engaging Students with 3D and Augmented Reality
- Escape This! Building Virtual Escape Rooms (for free!)
- Code Talkers: Utilizing Amazon's Echo in Your College Classroom
- Cyber Pathways Across Maryland (CPAM) Personal Adaptive Learning Solutions

Epitomizing it all was "There's an App for That? There's an App for That!" a session where participants were promised to leave with

> a number of apps that can be used in varying situations in both eLearning and traditional face-to-face classrooms. . . . At the end of the session you will:
>
> - Know how to search for apps that can achieve your intended goals
> - Be able to identify free or cheap apps for use in and out of the classroom
> - Have explored various apps and determined how they might be used.[13]

BLENDED LEARNING

As the multiple apps and alternative formats bleed from distance courses into the classroom, it is increasingly difficult to draw the boundaries between online instruction and the traditional classroom. Online courses increasingly include live chat rooms, video-centric discussions, and real-time gaming experiences. Regular classrooms often do the same. Most classrooms now post all the course materials online, have a digital textbook option, and require online activities and assignments.

Blended learning represents a formalization of this transition. Where a significant portion of the learning experience is in an online or remote video format, yet that percentage has not reached an arbitrary benchmark, the coursework may be referred to as *blended learning*. With the benchmark generally set by a state or governing board at 50%, 60%, or even as low as 30%, blended learning is particularly advantageous for working students who still need some of the structure of a classroom.

As a rule, blended classrooms still follow a strict schedule. Students are expected to meet at specific dates and at specific times, but the meetings occur less frequently than they would in a traditional class. Assignments generally are also due on a schedule that emulates the classroom but generally are submitted through the learning management system, by email, or through an online portal.

With the advent of desktop video, blended courses have taken a new format where students meet in a physical classroom for much of the semester while holding meetings via live Internet rooms on alternative weeks.

COLLABORATIVE ONLINE LEARNING

Project-based learning with students at multiple locations is an emerging classroom model enabled by the advances in electronic communications and the Internet of Things. As demonstrated by the SUNY Ulster case study, students with shared goals can accomplish much in a collaborative online environment.

Using tools such as Skype (www.skype.com), Blackboard Connect (https://teacher.blackboardconnected.com/), Adobe Connect (www.adobe.com/products/adobeconnect.html), or Zoom (www.zoom.us), the ability to work in groups across distances is greatly enhanced. Smaller groups can simply plan their work using a phone chat and texting.

Microsoft, Apple, and Google each incorporate a battery of collaboration tools, from their standard word processing package to foreign-language translation apps. As examples of the Internet of Things moving indiscreetly into society, the tools are used daily by millions.

CASE STUDY: COIL AT SUNY ULSTER AND GLASGOW CALEDONIAN UNIVERSITY

By Hope Windle, Anne M. J. Smith, and Julie C. Thomson

At the State University of New York (SUNY) at Ulster, the community college campus partners internationally to ensure that their students gain the skills needed for tomorrow's workforce. Where current employment often requires high levels of competency in team work, digital professionalism, and an ability to get work done virtually, internationally, and collaboratively, traditional classrooms find it a challenge to deliver such a multidimensional requirement normally met through student mobility and exchange programs.[a]

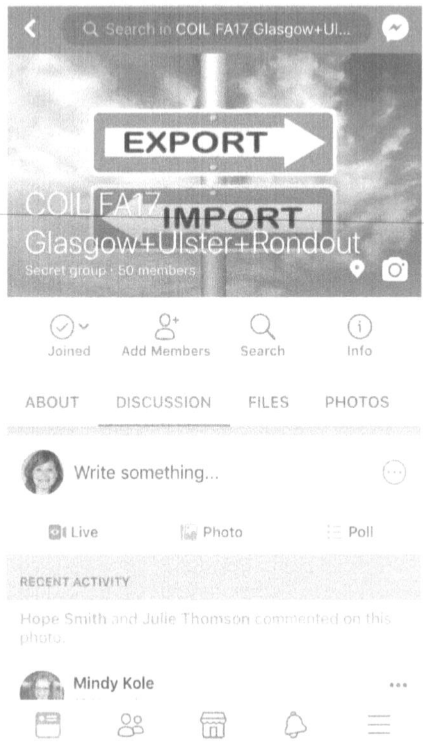

Figure 4.9. ***Facebook site COIL FA17 Glasgow+Ulster+Rondout***

Asked to deliver "work ready" graduates, how do institutions begin to prepare to teach students at low cost and in a technologically and internationally inclusive and accessible way? Working with the Glasgow School for Business and Society at Glasgow Caledonian University and with others, faculty at SUNY Ulster have found their solution by harnessing the power of the Internet.

Designed for collaboration, Internet-based tools have enabled crowd funding, open educational resources for writing and research, and crowd sourcing for collaborative inventions and engineering. Collaborative working between the two schools was harnessed using a variety of web platforms such as Google Drive (www.google.com/drive/) and Wikispaces (www.wikispaces.com).[b]

ACTIVITY

Offered under the acronym of COIL (Collaborative Online International Learning, www.coil.suny.edu), the State University of New York enables students to work on collaborative projects with college students in other countries. Working with counterparts in Scotland, SUNY, to import, export, and market retail products, students in both countries gain an understanding and appreciation for international business and marketing.

Piloting the online international enterprise trading project, Ulster College (SUNY) and Glasgow Caledonian University (GCU) first required their students to meet and to virtually establish a working relationship across cultures. Students followed up by researching the two markets and then buying products for their partners in the collaborating teams to sell. A process for importing and exporting the researched products was planned and implemented. Sales strategies were prepared. Finally, the products were sold.

In the process of assuring student collaboration, the higher education partners harnessed faculty collaboration to analyze the design principles and operationalization, resulting in culturally sensitive and value-added cost/outcomes.

As a result, project objectives were shaped, enabling the students to

- gain a preliminary understanding of how to work on business problems with people of another culture and
- develop important business and communication skills as well as a unique résumé addition that can set them apart from other job candidates.

Figure 4.10. Planning for the COIL project was often conducted via a Facebook discussion or through live Skype connections. *Facebook site COIL FA17 Glasgow +Ulster+Rondout*

The eight-week project harnessed an array of effective interactive platforms and applications for student engagement. Students from both institutions communicated using Facebook, Slack, and Skype, then collaborated on a report for their assessment. Students were monitored for developments in their cultural sensitivity as well as their understanding about innovation and entrepreneurship in the United States and Scotland.[c]

Individual module learning outcomes were met through experiential learning,[d] with the students demonstrating their new skills of developing entrepreneurial organizations through innovation practice in international settings. Not only did the participants increase their ability to meet the demands of cross-cultural teamwork but they also improved their knowledge of entrepreneurship, innovation, and trading across nations.

(continued)

CASE STUDY: COIL AT SUNY ULSTER AND GLASGOW CALEDONIAN UNIVERSITY *(continued)*

IMPLICATIONS

The pilot demonstrated that technologies can offer educational opportunities with an international dimension, which, due to time, mobility, and expense, were available to only a few students and staff. Now in its third year, the international collaborative trade project has been developed and honed.

Figure 4.11. Marketing their imports required the students to create an online catalog of the products. *Facebook site COIL FA17 Glasgow+Ulster+Rondout*

CONCLUSION

Performance in the 21st-century workplace is based on an ability to harness the power of Internet collaborations. It is clear that graduating students need to have engaged in real-world learning experience and practice with variant social and cultural protocols. Students also need to use and master a variety of collaboration platforms and applications. And finally, COIL demonstrated a need for the graduate to have the confidence and security to manage boundaries of social interaction and professional engagement in multicultural settings—essential strategies for professional practice.

The COIL collaboration between SUNY Ulster and Glasgow Caledonian University has demonstrated how the inextricable link between the Internet and collaborative working can be achieved in higher education at a low cost with diverse student groups across continents.

Hope Windle is the International Virtual Exchange COIL coordinator and an instructional design educator at the State University of New York (SUNY) at Ulster. She holds a master of fine art from the University of California, Davis.

Anne M. J. Smith and Julie C. Thomson are with the Glasgow School of Business and Society at Glasgow Caledonian University. Dr. Smith is a senior lecturer in business management with a PhD in entrepreneurial learning in agri-enterprise

Figure 4.12. ***Facebook site COIL FA17 Glasgow+Ulster+Rondout***

Figure 4.13. ***Facebook site COIL FA17 Glasgow+Ulster+Rondout***

from the Glasgow School for Business and Society. Dr. Thomson is a lecturer in business management with a PhD in innovation management from the University of the West of Scotland.

NOTES

a. British Council. 2015. *Broadening Horizons: The Value of the Overseas Experience*. London: British Council. United Kingdom Council for International Student Affairs (UKCISA). 2008. *Mobility Matters: Forty Years of UKCISA*. London: UKCISA. European Commission. 2014. *ERASMUS: Facts, Figures and Trends*. Brussels: European Commission.

b. Halcro, K., and A. M. J. Smith. 2011. "Wikis: Building Learning Experiences between Academe and Businesses." *Reflective Practice* 12 (5): 679–93.

c. Cooper, S. Y., and W. A. Lucas. 2007. "Building Entrepreneurial Self-Efficacy and Intent through Education and Experience." Proceedings of the 30th ISBE Institute for Small Business and Entrepreneurship Conference, Glasgow, Scotland, November 2007.

d. Kolb, D. A. 1984. *Experiential Learning: Experience as the Sources of Learning and Development*. Englewood Cliffs, NJ: Prentice Hall.

VIRTUAL LEARNING

The creation of learning experiences within augmented and virtual universes provides an entirely new and immersive opportunity for learners. Students access game- and entertainment-based worlds from an early age. For any learning that can be constructed within a competency-based environment, virtualization of the learning experience is generally possible.

Adventures in artificial intelligence are also offering the first steps for open-ended instruction, with students interacting with a computer-generated instructor, avatar, or programmed tutor that also learns with experience.

The suggestion that classrooms be constructed as serious games is implied, but there is more to this point. When teachers set clear expectations and allow students to chart their own route toward task completion, students learn to manage their own learning. In a more self-directed environment, they divide tasks, make decisions, and learn from the consequences of their actions.

In a white paper titled "Learning in the 21st Century,"[14] the International Education Advisory Board looked at the video game industry. Video games in many ways are addictive due to the characteristics that also make them ideal for the learning environment. The following are some of the more popular game characteristics:

- **Defined Goals**—Online games give the participants straightforward rules for how a game works and an exact definition of success with the game. Students will know how to play.
- **Reward Patience**—Digital gaming allows for repetition. Players can reenact a role or a task as many times as they need for practice and mastery. As many ways may be available to complete a task, players can make mistakes and repeat their work until they are successful.
- **Encourage Teams**—In the online gaming world, players who can work together have more opportunities to win. And just like Little League, many scenarios require the contestants to join a team in order to play. As collaboration in many games extends to online fan sites and discussion boards, college students will tap online resources related to their studies and enter class discussions through the learning management system or other sites.
- **Tracking**—Nearly every online game has levels of achievement, with players earning badges and moving up to the next stage with each round of success. Popular games like *Words with Friends* or *HQ* have become adept at adding rewards and player opportunities built upon the tracking of their players. In a learning environment, student mastery of a new skill can be tracked and communicated using the analytics from their Internet-based tools.

VIRTUAL WELDING—
FLORENCE-DARLINGTON TECHNICAL COLLEGE

By Derk Riechers

Welding, as with many other trades, requires hands-on experience to both master the trade and to understand how the welding gases and metals work together. At Florence-Darlington Technical College (FDTC), in the beautiful Pee Dee region of South Carolina, students can earn a certificate in applied science (CAS) in welding or participate in the college's shorter Pipe Welding Academy. The program is under the leadership of Director Jamie King, has 2 full-time instructors and 3 adjunct welding instructors, and 120 students.

Figure 4.14. A Lincoln Welding Simulator in use at Florence-Darlington Technical College. Notice the image seen by the welder in the video monitor on the upper right. *Courtesy Florence-Darlington Technical College*

(continued)

VIRTUAL WELDING—FLORENCE-DARLINGTON TECHNICAL COLLEGE *(continued)*

A constant challenge for the welding program has been the availability of resources and providing students with the latest technology in the field of study. Having a cool piece of technology is always fun to have in the classroom—but having technology that saves money and increases student success is another story entirely.

The machine that is currently being used in this academic department is a Lincoln Welding Simulator. Students can realistically virtualize shielded metal arc welding (SMAW) or gas metal arc welding (GMAW) on this simulator. In an SMAW scenario, a welder holds a rod to the point of the weld. GMAW uses a roll of wire to make the weld and also requires a tank of inert gas in the process.

FDTC has coupons for tee joints and pipe for students to weld, testing their welding skills. The students love it because it is easy to set up and start right away. If they make a bad weld, they can easily change coupons and keep welding.

The virtual welding machine helps students learn how to weld without all of the risk. During regular welding, there is always a possibly of burning your hand or arm. Burns are a serious concern, especially for a new student just learning the trade. Virtualization takes the risk out of the equation as students are introduced to the welding field. Struggling students, in particular, are assigned to the machine to gain confidence.

One of the other great benefits of the machine is cost. Because it's a virtual welder, this technology has eliminated the need for a large portion of the practice material and supplies. As a result, the department has been able to lower costs while still introducing welding to more students.

Beyond cost and safety, one of the greatest advantages of welding simulation may just be the students' reactions. Students love not getting burned, and they gain bragging rights as the machine provides an immediate score for each virtual weld. Of even more importance, having this piece of technology in the classroom gives the students a chance to readily apply a virtual skill set within the trade. Overall, using this technology within the trade has led the students to better understand the field of welding.

Derk Riechers is the chief operating officer and cofounder of Virtical Education (www.virticaled.com). Formerly with Florence-Darlington Technical College, he has recently joined Northeastern Technical College in Cheraw, South Carolina, as their director of dual enrollment and multi modalities. He holds a master of arts in human resource development, leadership, and management from Webster University and an MBA from Capella University.

- **Constantly Changing**—In the gaming environment, motion and change is constant. As a player moves through the game, new challenges are revealed, timed to match the newer skills gained in the process. Internet-based tools and analytics can create a parallel experience for learners, incorporating change as the students progress.
- **Immediate Consequences**—In a game, the consequence of an action, either good or bad, is felt immediately. The feedback function offered by Internet-enabled tools can keep your learners onboard as they see the impact of an action through grades, badges, or other feedback as the events unfold.
- **Personalization**—Tracking and the information-gathering function of games provides the opportunity for the Internet-based tools to completely personalize the experience for the player. Learners can enter an environment from a number of roles. In a virtual medical scenario, a student can perform as an anesthesiologist, a nurse practitioner, a records specialist, or an emergency medical technician, altering their perspective and honing a variety of skill sets.
- **Discernable Patterns**—As games are constructed around algorithms, patterns are inherent. By learning to detect the patterns, students gain skills in logic and application. Their success in applying logic and decision making in simulated but critical situations can bolster critical thinking and their mastery of a subject.

Virtual environments are replacing or extending the simulation options for students in both the online and the classroom setting. The impact is affecting how colleges plan for student access, lay out campus facilities, and even decide on what facilities are needed for the coming generation of students.

Before getting too far into the big picture, however, it might be good to visualize a few day-to-day academic options for capitalizing on the Internet of Things.

NOTES

1. CDW Government LLC. 2010. *CDW-G 2010 21st-Century Classroom Report.* Lincolnshire, IL: CDW. Retrieved from https://immagic.com/eLibrary/ARCHIVES/GENERAL//CDW_US/C100628C.pdf.

2. Moeller, Babette, Tim Reitzes, and Education Development Center (EDC). 2011. *Integrating Technology with Student-Centered Learning*, pp. 5–6. Quincy, MA: Nellie Mae Education Foundation. Retrieved from http://www.nmefoundation.org/getmedia/befa9751-d8ad-47e9-949d-bd649f7c0044/Integrating-Technology-with-Student-Centered-Learning?ext=.pdf.

3. United Nations Educational, Scientific, and Cultural Organization. 2015. "Proclamation of the 28th day of September as the International Day for the Universal Access to Information, 38 C/70," p. 1. *UNESCO 38th General Conference*. Retrieved from http://unesdoc.unesco.org/images/0023/002352/235297e.pdf. Accessible from https://en.unesco.org/iduai2017.

4. Maslow, A. H. 1943. "A Theory of Human Motivation." *Psychological Review* 50 (4): 370–96. doi:10.1037/h0054346. Citation from "Maslow's Hierarchy of Needs," Wikipedia, retrieved from https://en.wikipedia.org/wiki/Maslow%27s_hierarchy_of_needs.

5. College of Journalism and Communication, University of Florida. N.d. "History of Distance Education." Digital Media Lab. Retrieved from http://iml.jou.ufl.edu/projects/spring01/declair/history.html.

6. Zigerell, James. 1988. *The American Association of Community Colleges Instructional Telecommunications Consortium: The First Ten Years*. Washington, DC: Instructional Telecommunications Consortium.

7. Apple Computer. 1979. *Lemonade Stand.* Uploaded by Jason Scott to Historical Software Collection, Internet Archive, October 11, 2013. Retrieved from https://archive.org/details/Lemonade_Stand_1979_Apple.

8. Heick, Terry. 2017. "A Brief History of Video Games in Education." TeachThought. Updated September 8, 2017. Retrieved from https://www.teachthought.com/technology/a-brief-history-of-video-games-in-education/.

9. Knight, Daniel. 2014. "Personal Computer History, 1974–1984." Low End Mac, May 26, 2014. Retrieved from http://lowendmac.com/2014/personal-computer-history-the-first-25-years/.

10. Peterson's LLC. 2017. "The History of Online Education." November 2017. Retrieved from https://www.petersons.com/articles/online-degrees/online-education-history.

11. Lokken, Fred, and Mickey Slimp. 2017. "Evolving Strategies and Lessons Learned from the *Instructional Technology Council Annual eLearning National Survey*." Technology review, Community College Enterprise, Schoolcraft College, Fall 2017, 73–79.

12. Instructional Technology Council. 2018. "Schedule" [downloadable application]. eLearning 18. Available from Google Play.

13. Evins, Matthew, and Karl Frisch. 2018. "There's an App for That? There's an App for That!" eLearning2018, Instructional Technology Council Annual Conference, Tucson, AZ, February 11, 2018.

14. International Education Advisory Board (IAEB). 2013. "Learning in the 21st Century: Teaching Today's Students on Their Terms." IAEB white paper 040808. Retrieved from https://www.certiport.com/Portal/Common/DocumentLibrary/IEAB_Whitepaper040808.pdf.

Chapter Five

Smartphones and Student-Empowered Learning

"Before we go any further into today's discussion, everyone pull out your smartphone. If you left yours in your car or at home, move your desk over to your neighbor's to work in pairs."

Barry Tipton's class was one of the more enjoyable ones for Jordan. Following a high school program that immersed her in technology from day one, Dr. Tipton's class was more her norm.

"Class, today we're tackling photo sensors. What I want you to do is to write down two work fields or areas of study you would like to go into. Now, using the name of that area and adding a second term, photo sensors, *conduct a search to find something interesting to share with the class."*

The first of Jordan's classmates to speak up had searched on "baseball." In one article, the major leagues had chosen a company to provide "bat sensor"[1] *technology that would attach to a bat's handle. Getting into the most minute details of the batter's swing, a coach could combine the information with his or her smartphone video for a detailed examination of any issues. A second article highlighted related technologies in other sports, including a Bluetooth-enabled tennis racket that not only documented the swing but identified where the "ball connects with the racket strings."*[2] *Golf swings, row boat sculling, and other sports followed, with devices now even tracking basketballs and hockey pucks.*

Dr. Tipton added in that even though different from photo sensors, other sensor technologies had come into use with football. Inside their helmets, local high school students donned skull caps with built-in sensors to detect potential concussions. "Who would like to go next?" the professor queried.

Jordan was thinking about her baby brother, Johnny, when she selected her topic of child development. Johnny had just turned seven, and she was fascinated by how different he was now than just a few years ago.

Figure 5.1. Embedded sensors have changed the world of college athletics. From baseball bat and tennis racket attachments that track and record real-time motion to helmet implants that monitor impact, IoT provides analytics at an unprecedented scale. ***Courtesy of Mickey Slimp***

Her search opened a number of finds, but one in particular interested her: "Smart Toys Designed for Detecting Developmental Delays."[3] *The article noted, "By introducing sensors inside the toys, it will be possible to give the examiner more and better information to detect disorders in standard children. Consequently, the detection of developmental delays could improve their sensibility."*

Using wearable devices on their wrists and torsos, and with other sensors built into the diagnostic toys, motions were observed and tracked in the children in the study to detect Autism Spectrum Disorder (ASD).

As the second decade of the 21st century started, the majority of students were told to put away their personal electronic devices while in the classroom. Instead of seizing a chance to use tools the students already had, too many instructors saw opportunities for cheating. The very idea that students might be using that rich resource to find the answers rather than memorizing what was in some textbook was unthinkable.

The development of the smartphone and its integration within the daily routine of the student is a key component of the Internet of Things (IoT). Personal devices are already mainstays of distance and classroom-based instruction and will become essential as students lead the way into a *student empowered learning* environment.

How are teachers currently transforming phones from an interference with to an enabler of classroom instruction? By empowering students to identify interests and to pursue knowledge with their own personal device, they create an environment where students seek out answers and welcome challenges rather than merely attempting to memorize what someone else thought they should know.

SO MANY ~~TOYS~~ TOOLS

For young children, toys have always been a key element of learning. In the 20th century, children acted *upon* the toys they played with. When playing, the owner completely controlled the toy—placing and running it, talking to it in a one-way conversation, and using his or her imagination to bring the toy to life.

In the 21st century, toys have become interactive. Toys move independently, tell jokes, learn facts and preferences about the person handling it, and interact on a personal level. Many toys act in conjunction with a smart device. As children in this IoT world are mastering their tablet-type devices as infants, they adapt quickly to manipulating toys from their devices.

Toys have also become active far beyond their smart controls. Children's toys now learn words, respond to touch, and have facial expressions. A 10-year-old today grows up experiencing the reality of the Internet of Things in a way adults have not. Already, their expectations for education include smart devices in the classroom, from preschool through graduate education.

Figure 5.2. The Dino Cognitoy uses both IoT and artificial intelligence to become a more personalized toy for its child. Connected via Wi-Fi and the Internet to an AI core engine, Dino learns through each interaction. ***Courtesy of Mickey Slimp***

CogniToys.com, for example, is a product of a start-up company called Elemental Path, creating smart toys in the ultimate IoT fashion. Raising venture capital using Kickstarter (www.kickstarter.com),[4] the entrepreneurial group created Dino, a toy talking dinosaur that can interact with children.

Predating the popularization of Google Home and Echo Dot, and originally powered through IBM's Watson supercomputer, Dino could recall information about the children it interacted with, play games, help with spelling and math, tell jokes and stories, and more. Using the Internet interface, the owners are constantly upgrading the algorithms for the software based on the activities of and the interactions with users.

The tools and toys provided through the Internet of Things are integral to the future of learning and instruction. Incorporating the tools holds much promise for educators. How will this occur? Through the Center for Digital Education[5] and others, models are emerging. Here are some examples.

Class Research

Following Dr. Tipton's example in Jordan's vignette, smartphones are excellent tools for introducing students to the research behind a topic and initiating their involvement with a discussion. Information found from simple to complex online searches can open the door to a discussion on research validity, with an examination of what makes for a legitimate versus a questionable resource.

Social Media

Students are better than teachers at knowing what the current social apps are and, thus, should be included in a discussion of what is in current usage. Twitter and Facebook, of course, gained added notoriety from their political impact in the latter 2010s, while Instagram remains a tool more focused on millennials and Gen Z–age students.

Hashtags, used to identify discussion topics in Twitter or Instagram feeds, such as #eLearning2019, #sciencenews, or #latinoedu, can be shared with students to provide relevance and immediacy to knowledge feeds from current and emerging experts in a field. Pulling resources using a certain hashtag can be part of an assignment. A course-specific hashtag can also be created, such as #DTiptonsElectric201, to provide students with an easy way to share ideas and to generate discussion.

Texting

Why? Because email is so 2005. As hard as schools try, getting students to regularly check and use email is becoming more difficult. Communicating the most important course information by text ("Test this Friday!") is the most likely way to make sure the message reaches the student.

Emergency notifications, including school outages and criminal incidents on campus, are now available through apps integrated with the college's student information system.

Discussion Boards

Whether online or not, most courses now use learning management software (LMS) or a similar tool to enable structured and unstructured student discussions. Whether on Canvas, Blackboard, D2L, or Moodle, the system most likely has a phone app to give the student immediate access. For those not using an LMS, Twitter, Facebook, and other options for discussions are easily accessed.

Discussion boards allow students to explore content, improve their writing, and learn to express their ideas. Discussion prompts from faculty are generally appreciated, including an initial setting of the topic and suggestions when a topic drags or goes too deeply into a "rabbit hole."

Photography and Video Assignments

A cell phone camera can pull a student directly into his or her environment. Targeting instruction to include the use of student photos or small group videos can immerse learners into a topic, pulling the study topic into the real world.

Encourage or require students to place pictures within their essays. Create a class site in your LMS or on Pinterest (www.pinterest.com) for posting their work. Use YouTube (www.youtube.com) to post final class video projects. Engage your students in scavenger hunts with a list of assignment-related photos or videos to collect. Allow them to collect images online or provide extra credit for original work.

A popular app project related to scavenger hunts is Geocaching (www.geocaching.com). Geocaching can focus on a location almost anywhere and sends students on a search to find it using their GPS. When they arrive, they find a small container holding a "log book," where they can sign in and comment. Geocaching around a historic or geological site can result in an interesting writing assignment and provide students with a common experience.

Student Polling

Polling students, using tools like SurveyMonkey, Poll Everywhere, or survey tools within an LMS, allows course participants to remain engaged in the discussion through physical action and immediate responses. Whether in the classroom or within a virtual space, the immediate feedback polling tools offer gives the teacher an insight into how students are comprehending a topic while helping students maintain a focus on the subject.

Making a Call

With a phone in their hand, the world is literally at the students' fingertips—and yours. With a little preplanning, students can bring anyone, anywhere into a course discussion. Set up an appointment through your textbook vendor to arrange for the students to call the textbook author from the classroom or tagged into the online discussion group. Use the phone to bring area professionals into the class, adding real-world examples to classroom studies. Enable students to regularly identify and bring in an expert—even just for a few minutes—for a discussion on a classroom topic.

Recording

The recording capability built into phones makes for another teaching and learning tool. Obviously, the cell phone can become a simple recording device to capture lectures and class discussions. But everything mentioned previously or in the remainder of this list can be recorded in advance. Then it can be brought into the course by the teacher or student at a relevant moment.

Interviews and Oral History

The simplicity and complexity built into a phone offers students a powerful tool for bringing a topic to life. Collecting stories of their grandparents' Cold War experiences, memories of the first Moon landing, or their parents' recollections of 9/11 can pull students directly into their studies. As a group project, students can be taught to script and edit their collections into semester reports.

Foreign Language and Intercultural Exchange

Today's Internet tools and apps provide an unprecedented means to practice second-language vocabulary and conversation. Apps like HelloTalk (www.hellotalk.com), HiNative (www.hinative.com), Bilingua (https://bilingua.io/), or Tandem (www.tandem.net) will even partner students with a native speaker to barter conversations in the language of choice for practice in using English with a second-language speaker.

Online gaming in another language is another great route to intercultural immersion. Foreign-language children's games, such as those offered on Nick Jr. France (www.nickelodeonjunior.fr), or even common English-language games like *Call of Duty: Black Ops* (http://store.steampowered.com/agecheck/app/311210/) played with an alternate language option offer great practice.[6] Websites like FluentU (www.FluentU.com) offer numerous options and ideas for engaging in other languages and cultures.

IS LEARNING CHANGING DUE TO IOT?

So what do all of the new options for learning mean for higher education, its classrooms, and tomorrow's students? The routes for tomorrow's leaders are changing in real time, and the knowledge and choices for school direction are rapidly moving.

INTERVIEW: WALTER CHEEK, BREAKAWAY GAMES

BreakAway Games started as an entertainment gaming company creating recreational battle games. Picked up by the U.S. Department of Defense, they evolved into what is called "serious gaming," creating virtual scenarios where learners were dropped into alternative worlds for realistic simulation.

They now have a variety of clients and games, ranging from dental care to genetics to engine repair, where learners are immersed into an alternate universe for learning.

Walter Cheek, Breakaway Ltd.'s vice president of business development, has made his career identifying new venues for 21st-century students.

WHAT DOES BREAKAWAY DO, AND HOW HAS THAT CHANGED THE NATURE OF EDUCATION AND TRAINING?

We started building entertainment products. And even though that was the original intent, the very first project this company did was to build a theater-level wargame for the Office of the Secretary of Defense Net Assessment.

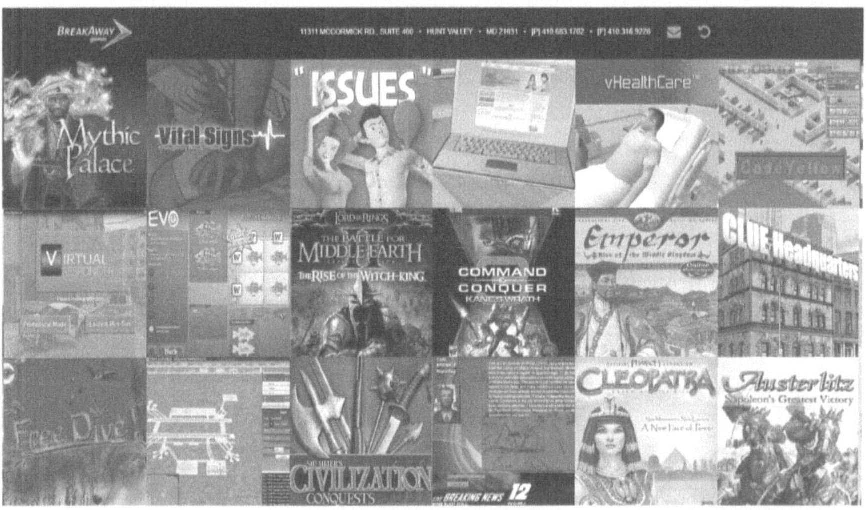

Figure 5.3. BreakAway Games started as an entertainment gaming company creating recreational battle games. Picked up by the U.S. Department of Defense, they evolved into what is called serious gaming, creating virtual scenarios where learners were dropped into alternative worlds for realistic simulation. They now have a variety of clients and games, ranging from dental care to genetics to engine repair, where learners are immersed into an alternative universe for learning. Walter Cheek, Breakaway's vice president of business development, has made his career identifying new venues for 21st-century students. *Courtesy of Breakaway, Ltd.*

Developing technology is not hard. I think it's actually easy. Going from the idea and then into a working prototype and then into a finished product. Assimilation is the issue. In the education world, how do you get people who are doing a good job and are comfortable with what they are doing, how do you help them change?

Looking at adoption curves, the one that everybody wants is the cell phone. In education, the typical innovation takes 10 to 15 years to deploy. Getting others to buy in and use something is a slow process. In education, people feel like they know what they're doing, so why change?

HAS THIS CHANGED WITH SERIOUS GAMING?

People want game technology because they think this will make students want to learn and they will enjoy it. Well, no. Watching my son grow up, I can't tell you how many controllers were thrown against the wall out of sheer frustration. His desire was to beat the game. Calling that enjoyable is a misnomer. Saying that he was engaged in this and by sheer brute force he was going to win and consequently learn is interesting, because he was.

One "aha moment" was when my son was playing a Star Wars game and said his favorite weapon was a shoulder-mounted rocket launcher. I said you don't need that in that game because there's nothing flying around.

He said, "Dad, I don't care. I can kill 10,000 bots with one shot. I get the highest kill rate using a weapon made for something else."

What he showed me was a couple of things. One, he was thinking very creatively about what would work best for what he was trying to accomplish. As a 10-year-old kid, he was able to choose an unconventional tool to meet the goal he had set.

Another time, when he was building a sword, he said to me, "Dad, I want to buy some golf clubs. Can we go to a golfing store?" So we go to a store and he says, "Show me some Tiger Woods clubs." As we look at them, he says, "These are called *blades*, right, Dad?" Then, "Okay—so now I understand."

What he understood was the difference between a golf club that was cast and a golf club that was forged. From his game, this 10-year-old boy started understanding some of the fundamentals of metallurgy. In his game, he built swords out of steel and out of cast iron. He now knew which was stronger and was easily repaired. So he chooses the alloy to make steel swords out of. You suddenly have a 10-year-old kid who actually understands metallurgy without knowing what the word is. That's incredibly powerful.

Now, if you look at a field like health care, all of a sudden I have to figure out how to replace at least the 50% of the people who are going to retire in the next 10 years. But how do I impart the knowledge of a 30-year-old nurse into a 22-year-old in under 30 years? That's the issue.

We can use gaming technology. I can use the technology that has been developed more for just pure entertainment and put that into a learning system. Not

(continued)

only can I have people play, I can also collect the results of the game to improve the outcomes.

Today, I go to school and get a diploma and my diploma says I'm something. And I get that diploma because I passed a bunch of tests. I didn't necessarily do the real-world experience.

The first day you sit down at a new job, you will not be as efficient as you were on your old job. Because when you walked into your old job, you did certain things. You did them because you have that sort of muscle memory. These are the types of things that happen this time of year, this day of the week, and so forth. And so you go do those and then you start to deal with the things that are out of the ordinary.

So how do I get a CFO to go from a CFO to the CEO? In the new role, there's a period where the person cannot really work on auto pilot for some portion of what they're doing. They're probably thinking and overthinking on everything that they do.

So how do I get somebody through that? Because I know they have the capability, I know they have the experience. They have all the things that I want them to have. I have to get them through this first month or two because I don't want them to quit.

A university hospital CEO recently told me, "Our mentoring program is six to nine months depending on the individual. And I have an attrition rate today that's about 35%. As you think about it, that's a lot of money, and I have to be able to bring in a phenomenal amount of people just to stay at a steady state." Unless something changes, he is going to have to push more people through an existing system than it currently has the capability for.

As far as education today, it's hard to believe how out of step the business and the education communities are. They're completely out of step.

How do I get them to make that change?

At a conference we went to, a doc sat down next to me and said, "What are you doing?"

And I said, "I'm just looking at something we've built."

And he said, "Can I see it?" So I showed it to him. He goes, "I really like this stuff," and I said, "Why?"

And he goes, "Well, I can get my students to fail enough times that they begin to really understand the importance of the decisions they make in every step of the process. And the reason they understand that is because they understand what happens in failure."

So if I can do that, that's what I'm trying to do, to take someone out of college and have them be competent the day they walk in the door. We need to be able to get the requirements from industry more closely aligned with what's being taught in the school. It's about the doing of it. It isn't about the knowledge. It's about the ability to apply the knowledge.

NOTES

1. Shaw, S. Garrett. 2016. "Tech & Media: MLB Makes Blast Motion Official Bat Sensor Technology Provider." *Sports Illustrated*, July 1, 2016. Retrieved from https://www.si.com/tech-media/2016/07/01/mlb-blast-motion-bat-sensor-technology.

2. Lightman, Karen. 2016. "Consumer Electronics: Next-Gen Sensors Make Golf Clubs, Tennis Rackets, and Baseball Bats Smarter than Ever." *IEEE Spectrum*, posted February 25, 2016. Retrieved from https://spectrum.ieee.org/consumer-electronics/gadgets/nextgen-sensors-make-golf-clubs-tennis-rackets-and-baseball-bats-smarter-than-ever. This article appears in the March 2016 print issue of *IEEE Spectrum* as "Silicon Gets Sporty."

3. Rivera, Diego, Antonio Garcia, Bernardo Alarcos, Juan R. Velasco, Jose Eugenio Ortega, and Isaias Martinez-Yelmo. 2016. "Smart Toys Designed for Detecting Developmental Delays." *Sensors* 16 (11): 1–22. Retrieved from http://www.mdpi.com/1424-8220/16/11/1953/htm.

4. Kickstarter, PBC. 2018. "CogniToys: Internet-Connected Smart Toys That Learn and Grow." Retrieved from https://www.kickstarter.com/projects/cognitoys/cognitoys-internet-connected-smart-toys-that-learn.

5. Bentley, Kipp. 2017. "9 Uses for Smartphones in the Classroom." *Converge*, January 2, 2017. Retrieved from http://www.centerdigitaled.com/blog/cellphones-in-classrooms-part-2.html.

6. Stimola, Maureen. 2018. "Learn or Die! 5 Epic Ways to Learn Languages by Playing Video Games." *FluentU* blog. Retrieved from https://www.fluentu.com/blog/language-learning-video-games/.

Chapter Six

The Campus Network

So far, you have learned what the Internet of Things (IoT) is, where it came from, and how it may change life between now and 2030. Lives will change for individuals at large and, in particular, for students over the next two decades.

Classroom changes and models of instruction that will move colleges into the future were identified. With IoT integrated into the traditional, blended, and distance classrooms, new instructional models are also emerging, taking students into collaborative and experiential settings without regard to distance or physical facilities.

Several IoT pioneers have joined your journey, adding insights into classroom applications in health care, workforce technology, business and marketing, and intercultural studies. You have also delved deeply into the creativity of the emerging educational world, with inventors of serious gaming and virtual simulations and the builders of IoT-driven toys of the coming generations.

So as the educational leaders responsible for directing this change, what does IoT mean for the campus itself and for the facilities of the 2020s and 2030s? The Internet of Things is impacting how colleges

- collect and process information;
- choose and deploy services;
- direct the money flow;
- repurpose and restructure campus facilities;
- strategically acquire, move, and discard inventory;
- maximize energy and related resources; and
- foster campus security.

From the students' perspective, all of the components of IoT and of the campus itself should be working together seamlessly. As a campus is indeed a bureaucracy and normally functions within the larger bureaucracy of a state, community, or university system, things may never be perfect. Yet appropriately embedded technology within the physical structure of the campus offers an option for much greater efficiencies. The core infrastructure for making everything occur is the college network.

THE PHYSICS OF THE INTERNET

A dictionary definition of *the Internet* is "a global computer network providing a variety of information and communication facilities, consisting of interconnected networks using standardized communication protocols."[1] If this sounds confusing, keep reading. These terms are detailed in more depth to give you a greater understanding.

Synonyms for *the Internet* include *the World Wide Web*, *WWW*, *cyberspace*, *the Net*, *the information superhighway*, and *the infobahn*. You may have heard a few others. But it is pretty much the same thing—computers interconnecting across a distance and sharing information.

So how does the World Wide Web or WWW work? Simply put, users contract with an Internet service provider (also known as an ISP) to gain a route into the Internet. Where do Internet service providers exist? There are hundreds. The most common are telephone companies and cable television companies. Major corporations and universities or regional collaborations may even create their own Internet service provider, but it is an intricate proposition to become and maintain the access point and service.

There are also independent Internet service providers, but most local businesses, small colleges and universities, and local residents will contract either through a telephone company, a cable provider, or a regional collaborative. These companies will provide the equipment needed to bring the Internet signal to your home or to the edge of your educational or business network.

What is the difference between the telephone company and the cable company in terms of Internet access? Although the topography and technology are constantly changing, telephone companies traditionally furnished Internet service over their legacy copper wiring, which provides the dial tone and connection for a home telephone (also known as a *landline*). The service is termed *digital subscriber line* or *DSL*. Until recently, connection speeds over DSL have been limited, but new developments have quadrupled or quintupled that speed.

Cable companies typically provide Internet connections through the television cable connected to a home. In the past, this copper cable (called *coaxial cable* or *coax*) provided greater speeds than the telephone copper line. Many homes in urban and suburban areas use a cable provider for Internet access.

More recently, both cable and phone companies are installing fiber-optic lines to provide faster connection speeds. Since 2010, major federal projects, such as the Federal Communications Commission–subsidized Rural Health Care and E-Rate Programs, the Broadband Technologies Opportunities Program (BTOP), and more, have poured billions into upgrading, moving the national infrastructure from copper to fiber optics. Partnering colleges, hospitals, and K–12 schools with a variety of ISPs, millions of students have benefitted from improved access over the past 15 years. Today, far more campuses are connected via fiber, providing greater speeds and uninterrupted access.

ALWAYS CONNECTED

If there is one takeaway you gain from researching the Internet of Things at the college level, it should be the need to always stay connected. With requirements not so far afield from those in a robotic surgical suite, the college has a multitude of operations, equipment, and services in need of constant connectivity. In today's world, you must always have one or more backup sources of connectivity when your connection dies. This hits a campus at several levels.

Say the year is 2030 and a fleet of 1,000 Internet-controlled 18-wheelers are traveling an interstate over a five-mile stretch. Spaced 30 yards or 50 kilometers apart, each multiton semi is perfectly paced with the vehicles around it, rolling along at 90 miles per hour (speeds can be increased when everything is synchronized and substantially fueled by electricity or hydrogen).

Suddenly, the Internet signal is lost, either due to severe weather or a malicious hacker, even as an act of cyber warfare. With speed and direction no longer controlled, mayhem follows. Trucks roll and skid in every direction. The impacts are deadly and, with a tenth of the trailers carrying chemicals and hazardous materials, explosions, massive property damage, and environmental destruction follows.

Yet the nightmare scenario can and will be avoided. How?

Backup. The Internet signal controlling the trucks will be connected in multiple ways. Prior to robotic vehicles becoming routine, technologies are being put into place to ensure constant control and constant connectivity.

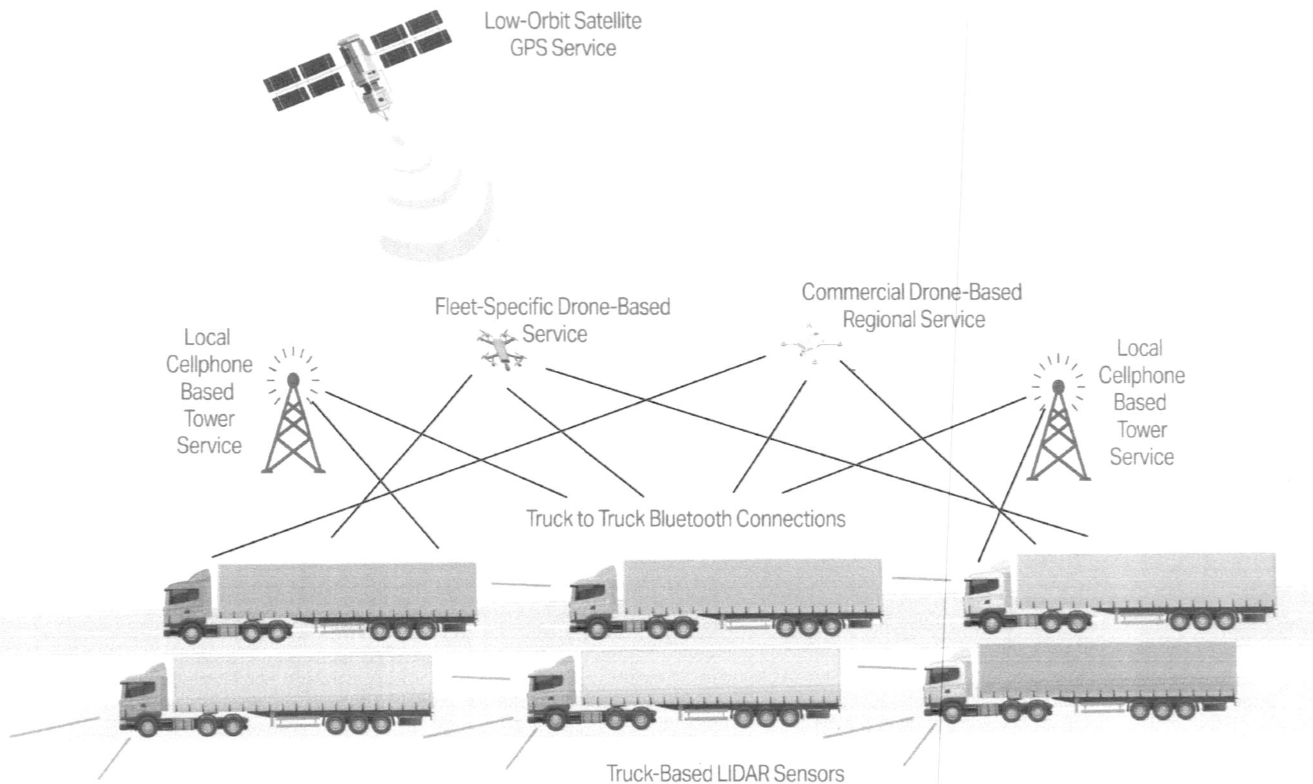

Figure 6.1. **Roadside redundancy. The technology infrastructure required for autonomous self-driving trucks must provide redundant navigational tools, simultaneously connected via Internet, Bluetooth, and wireless Ethernet, while truck-based cameras, laser-based radar (LIDAR), and even newer technologies add to their safety. The school of 2030 will require similar connections.** ***Courtesy of Kevin and Mickey Slimp***

In the prerobotic era, wireless connections occurred haphazardly along the highway. When a cell phone tower was in your line of sight, your phone remained connected. As you crossed over a hill, the signal was lost. Driving between towering buildings on a major city street, your signal was sporadic at best.

Robotic cars and trucks will gain their signals in a variety of ways. First, there is the traditional cell tower. Next, satellite services will provide both GPS mapping and instruction from low earth orbit. In high-traffic areas or locations with complicated terrain, drones carrying cell antennas can be deployed.

Backup will also be built in at a vehicular level. Prior to losing the connection, the onboard guidance system would have downloaded the most recent maps of the area it was approaching. Multidirectional cameras on the truck cab and trailer would connect to image-recognition programming designed to respond to a preselected route and respond to emergency situations. Radar, or a newer laser-based technology known as LIDAR, emanating from the truck itself would control braking, speed, and maneuvering to continue the trip or to pull off of the road for safety.

In addition to being connected, the trucks themselves have become *intelligent devices*. An intelligent device is any object that has a computing capability built into it. The computing capacity gives the device an ability to make decisions and to network with other devices.

Should a signal fade or fail, the most recent data downloaded by the truck will continue guiding the routes, combined with the truck's own data collection and sensory inputs providing for adjustments. The truck would also be equipped with a laser-based radar-like technology, spotting moving objects and hazards in the immediate area and, through processing built into the truck's data system, adjusting accordingly. As a rule, data collected by the device is transmitted to the surrounding vehicles while also being delivered to a remote server for further coordination, evaluation, and planning.

Over the next two decades, the network coordination for a college campus will require a similar sophistication in its structure for Internet support. As students bring additional devices to campus and technology is embedded in the devices and applications throughout the organization, the requirements for your basic Internet connectivity and for redundancy in the ways that you connect will expand exponentially.

A rural Texas campus working with one of the authors recently faced this issue. With only one networking and Internet provider in the community, the nursing campus was 40 miles by a single fiber line from the parent institution. Services to the campus depended on a telecommunications vendor that subcontracted the smaller site to the company owning the fiber line.

The topography of the service resulted in a number of "single points of failure" that could and have isolated the nursing campus. When a fiber-line cut created an outage of nearly a day while repair crews were assembled and deployed, it was inconvenient. When an equipment failure required two days as the providers isolated the problem, jockeyed over whose equipment was responsible, and then prescribed and implemented a fix, it became annoying.

Then, when a software problem created an outage that took more than three days to isolate and repair, campus services took a major hit. Although some older employees recalled how to work in a "pencil and paper" environment, a number of the staff and faculty were at a loss. Payments to and from the campus were delayed, some classes were canceled, and a number of faculty and staff returned home or to another campus to work as they could.

COLLEGE AS CONNECTIVITY

With the advent of online degree programs, hybrid classes, virtual support services, and home communications, it can almost be argued that anywhere you can have a connection, you can have a college. If it were only so simple. The Rosseau ideal[2] of a teacher as a one-on-one, completely individualized coach and tutor has been brought closer with IoT but only with a significant degree of infrastructure support and connectivity.

The counterpoint is that wherever you have a college, you must have Internet. And just like with the autonomous robotic trucking company, the college needs to be supported by using multiple networking technologies with redundant, protected providers.

Who provides Internet to your college? As you point out a commercial provider, AT&T, CenturyLink, Comcast, or Altice come to mind as some of the major commercial players in the U.S. market. You also may be working with a state or regionally funded "research and education network" (REN), such as MERIT in Michigan, CENIC in California, NYSERNet in New York, or ARE-ON in Arkansas. Likewise, you may be partnering with a university system that has constructed its own independent network.

If your college is connected to any one of the aforementioned providers, you have made a mistake. Like the rural nursing campus just mentioned, a single fiber cut, equipment failure, or software glitch can put you out of service. But if you are connected to at least two and preferably three of the same or similar providers, using discrete fiber or wireless routes, you are starting to get the picture and are in a much better shape.

A campus located on a coastal island offers an obvious example. For a number of years, LEARN, Texas's research and education network, sought to provide expanded Internet services to the campuses on Galveston Island. Galveston is separated from the mainland by about a mile of the intercoastal waterway.

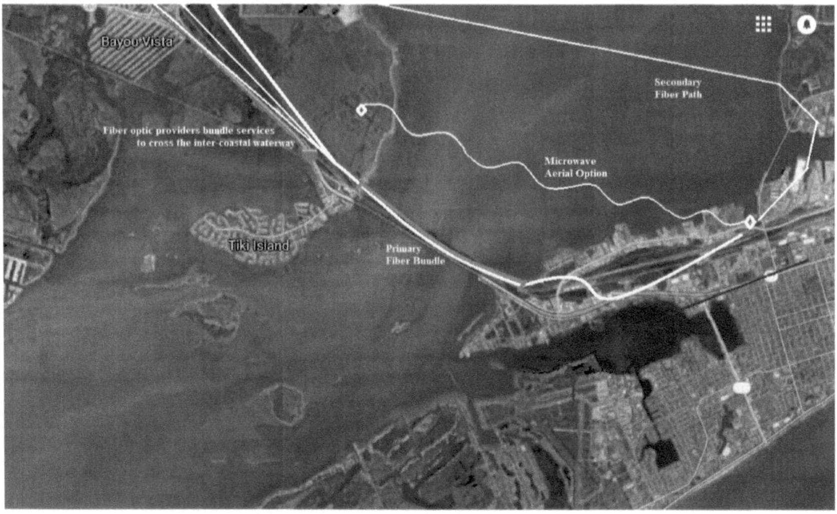

Figure 6.2. The challenge of providing protected Internet routes onto an island illustrates the challenge of supporting an isolated campus with limited providers. Without options, a single point of failure can shut down many of the campus systems. *Original satellite image generated from Google Maps, https://www.google.com/maps/place/Galveston+Island/. Note that the image does not represent actual and exact fiber and signal pathways.*

As the commercial services to the city bundled together for this last mile to reach the island, passing through a single conduit across the water created the potential for a single source of failure for the service. That is, a cutting of the fiber-optic line itself or a break with flooding inside of the conduit would cut off all of the network's Internet traffic.

What were the options? A second conduit from another end of the island was commercially available but would have added a significant expense for the service, and it was beyond what was available from the budgeted funds. A lower-speed aerial microwave signal could also have provided a layer of protection but was likewise costly and would provide less bandwidth.

With a major campus-based hospital dependent on the service and with the threat of coastal storms and hurricanes an annual event, a funding source for the secondary path was later found.

An isolated rural campus, however, can face much the same issue but with fewer options and resources. When a community lacks a commercial base (translation: not enough homes or businesses in a concentrated area) to support multiple Internet providers, a campus may be restricted to a single telecommunications provider or source. A publicly funded REN may step in but as often as not for more isolated sites, will be riding in the same bundle of fiber as the local commercially available service.

To ensure that a college has the connections it needs requires more than knowing who the providers originating the services are. You also have to have a reasonable concept of the physical pathway they follow to get to you. You need to know if your contractors acquire their "middle mile" or "long haul" service coming to your site over a common fiber bundle or through a shared conduit at any point along the way. If so, then you will need to take that into consideration to determine if your routes supply true redundancy and sufficiently protect your service.

Clemson University is located 30 miles outside of Greenville-Spartanburg, South Carolina, and is more than 120 miles from either Atlanta, Georgia, to the west or Charlotte, North Carolina, to the northeast. The city of Clemson is pretty much the college. With an enrollment of more than 24,000, the university's population is nearly 70% larger than the 14,000 permanent residents of the city, including faculty and local students.

Like Greenville-Spartanburg itself, however, this otherwise rural community is booming with education and technology. Connectivity and an aggressive embrace of technology has been key. Clemson's structure for its "wide-area network" (WAN) has stationed the college and the community to embrace the demands of an IoT age.

> The Clemson University LAN is connected to (or peers with) multiple other networks in various regional geographical locations with the goal of transporting data and communications around the world quickly and efficiently.
>
> Clemson peers with several commodity, or commercial, internet service providers (ISP) in addition to a national research and education (R&E) network called Internet2. Peering with multiple providers is an industry standard to ensure redundancy and business continuity in the event of a network outage for one or more ISPs. R&E networks were constructed to serve the R&E community on a member-only access policy to allow the faster and presumably more secure exchange of data between members over the network.
>
> Currently, Clemson's WAN peering locations include: Atlanta, GA, Charlotte, NC, Anderson, SC, and Clemson, SC. Clemson's commodity peers include: CenturyLink, Hurricane Electric, and Charter Communications. Clemson has two Internet2 peering points, one in Atlanta, GA and the other in Charlotte, NC. Total WAN bandwidth is currently 110 Gb/s to Atlanta and 10Gb/s to Charlotte. Clemson's facilities-based fiber network that runs between Atlanta, GA, Clemson, SC, Greenville, SC, and Charlotte, NC, called C-Light, has the capability to increase this bandwidth in either direction as needed by the Clemson University users.[3]

A smaller or midsized community college and regional university would hesitate to invest in and build the infrastructure described by Clemson. The demands of embedded technology and online programs, however, are changing the priorities for many. As enrollments have declined in traditional classroom offerings at many schools, a similar level of service could be constructed or acquired at the cost of erecting and operating a new building. With eLearning now making up 25% or more of many schools' enrollments, it may be a necessary investment.

SO HOW MUCH IS ENOUGH?

Moving past the discussion of network reliability and speed, the ongoing cost must consider network usage, needs, and Internet capacity.

As the Internet emerged in the 1990s, desktop computers connected to a telephone line using a modulator/demodulator or modem to connect to a POTS line, humorously named for a plain old telephone system. Fax machines, where used, still work that way, using an analog signal to transmit information. Modems originally connected at 14.4 kilobytes per second (kB/s) or 14,400 bytes.

A byte is roughly equivalent to one alpha character; for example, the letter *z* is one byte. Today, connection speeds are measured in megabytes (million bytes) per second and gigabytes (billion bytes) per second. With the storage capacity of computer hard drives now in the terabytes (trillion bytes), similar network capacities will soon follow.

With the emerging Internet of Things and personal demands for Internet-based entertainment, the need for faster connection speeds has exploded. Homes accessing and downloading online movies, music, and games are moving past the 200+ channels offered by satellite or cable. Rather than anteing up for traditional cable, millennial viewers are switching to one or more online services, such as Netflix, Hulu, or Amazon Prime, to buy only what they want to watch at a lower price—another benefit of the Internet of Things.

This is generating a much greater demand for higher connection speeds. A typical online movie requires a minimum of four megabits per second (eight megabits = one megabyte) for low-resolution picture and sound. For higher resolution (high definition or HD) and surround sound, connection speeds of 10 Mbps are required. Ultra-high definition (4K or UHD, now available on online video players and newer televisions) requires even more speed to deliver the quality picture and sound the equipment is capable of producing.

As users in the home or classroom simultaneously use additional devices or applications, the demand for speed goes higher or the quality of the service declines. In a home with a 10 Mbps or smaller connection, pictures delivered via iPhone, multiple emails coming in at once, or a second computer coming online will compete for bandwidth, causing a movie viewing to break up or delay until the competing activity abates.

For homes and small businesses near a city, speed, capacity, and usage is normally not an issue. Cable providers advertise a 100 Mbps (megabit per second) download speed as adequate for all of the connections in your home. Download speed governs what you access on the web. Watching high-definition or ultra-high-definition movies, for example, may require a ½ to 4 Mbps download speed. Upload speed governs what you send to the web. Typically, this is email or perhaps a few photos uploaded to the cloud. A 10 Mbps upload speed is plenty for most users.

Video gamers add to the load, with each player in the home expanding the need by 1 to 3 Mbps. Virtual reality and 360-degree motion panoramic videos may subsume your network requirements, with estimates for the future requiring 500 Mbps or more per headset.[4] But not yet.

Broadband is currently defined by the Federal Communications Commission as Internet connection speeds at or above 25 Mbps. In most urban and near-urban areas of the United States, 100 Mbps broadband is available. Most campuses are targeting connection speeds at one gigabit or greater to offer reliable wireless service to hundreds of employees and thousands of students.

Consider a small college campus with maybe 2,000 students at any one time. Guessing that each student carries a laptop, a tablet, a smartphone, and perhaps a smartwatch, it is possible to have 6,000 or more devices vying for the college network download speed and capacity. For a location with residence halls, the number of devices would increase to include televisions, gaming consoles, and perhaps specialty devices like graphic-design tablets. Other bandwidth-hungry applications could be in use, like photo- or video-editing software. Each device periodically reaches out to the web for updates, even when idle.

While today the number-one application used in college residence halls is Netflix, it could change at any time to become Hulu, Amazon Prime, another streaming service, or an up-and-coming game app. Whatever becomes popular will come preinstalled on almost everything, from tablets to smartphones to smart televisions. With voice-activated searching now available on most devices, a student can plop down in his or her dorm room, say "start TV" and "Russell Crowe," and bring up all of the movies that include this star.

"Schoolwork? Pfft . . . let's watch a movie first. It's only 10:00 p.m. after all."

The reality is that many campuses struggle to keep up with demand, especially on the campus wireless network. Hardly anyone connects with a wire any more. So how much is enough? Recommendations are for one gigabyte per 1,000 students, but reality paints a different picture. A typical residence hall with 150 students may have only 250 Mb of speed, hardly enough to satisfy hungry devices vying for the connection. In an ongoing battle, the end point will keep moving ahead.

With all these devices and individuals connecting, how does the information know where to go? Like your own mailing address, a number unique to

The Internet of things:

Bandwidth Recommendations & Reality	
Recommended	Reality
1 Gbps/1000 students	50 Mbps to 10 Gbps per College
By 2025	
1 Gbps/400 students	5 Gbps to 100 Gbps per College

Figure 6.3. Bandwidth recommendations for college campuses will continue to grow as the number of devices and apps per student continue to expand. ***Courtesy of Roy Bartels and Mickey Slimp***

you is assigned to your device or computer. That unique number follows a certain pattern or protocol. Here is how that works.

INTERNET PROTOCOLS

The world is a big place, and in order for everyone to communicate, standardizing computer-to-computer communication was essential. A protocol had to be established, giving each network-connected device a unique identifier or an "IP address," enabling other computers to "find" it, and enabling it to talk with other computers. Known as "Internet protocol" or IP, care has to be taken not to confuse the acronym with ISP, an Internet service provider, which is a totally different thing.

By using a common Internet protocol, the computer's platform and related operating systems (the most common examples are Windows and MacOS) are suddenly made agnostic. The standards set by IP enable communication between all computers, regardless of the operating system, manufacturer, origin, or type of device.

Internet protocol provides a basic set of instructions for transferring packets of data between computers. A packet is a small amount of data sent over the Internet or another network. IP delivers information to your computer as a series of individual packets, with each identifying the origination site, destination, and the information that connects it to other packets. Billions of packets are exchanged each day, with each reaching its destination in only a few seconds.

IPV4 AND IPV6

Take a look at how those identifiers are constructed. An IP address is the unique identifier for your particular networked device. Two IP address protocols now exist—IPv4 and IPv6.

The most common Internet protocol is IPv4 (Internet protocol version 4). This protocol looks like this: 123.123.123.123. Each set of three digits can accommodate a number from 0 to 255, giving a total number of IPv4 addresses at just over 4 billion.

Yet with billions and trillions of packets moving back and forth, concerns have risen that the Internet will run out of unique identifiers at some point. With an estimated 6 billion people in the world, and many people using more than one Internet-connected device, you can quickly see 4 billion IP addresses are inadequate. Do you even know how many Internet-connected devices you have? One author of this book, who lives alone, counted 22 Internet-connected devices in his home. The 2017 population of the United States was approximately 326 million. If only 30% of the population had 22 devices, that's over 2 billion devices.

A newer protocol is IPv6, Internet protocol version 6. Just coming into wider use, this protocol is quickly becoming a necessity. Placed on top of rather than replacing IPv4, IPv6 is being introduced as new devices come onto the market or as colleges and other sites expand their networks. IPv6 is also called *IPng*, for *Internet protocol–next generation.*

IPv6 allows for substantially more addresses than IPv4. IPv6 is typically described with the format: hhhh:hhhh:hhhh:hhhh:hhhh:hhhh:hhhh:hhhh, where each *h* can be replaced with either a letter or a number. Each set of four characters can be written using the numbers 0–9 and alpha characters from *A* to *F*, which uses a hexadecimal or base 16 numbering system—that is, each individual character can be filled with one of 16 options. A typical IPv6 address could look like F704:0000:0000:0000:3458:79A2:D08B:4320.

The newer IP has two related benefits. IPv6 creates a huge number of new addresses, which offers substantially greater security.

IPv6 can accommodate up to 32 trillion trillion trillion possible combinations (also known as *undecillion*), making it unlikely that the Internet will run out of addresses until at least midcentury. Nonetheless, the growth of personal and IoT-related embedded devices calls for caution with such predictions.

Security is built into the complexity of the new addresses. With such complex addresses, it is highly unlikely that a particular IP address can be "discovered" or "guessed." Continued attacks on campus networks and attempts by hackers to break into or disable networks will speed up the move to IPv6.

STATIC VERSUS DYNAMIC ADDRESSES

As any gamer can tell you, an object in motion, and particularly an object in random motion, is harder to hit than a target that stays in place. To offer a more secure environment, IP addresses, in either IPv4 or IPv6, can take advantage of a similar attribute. IP addresses can be established as either static or dynamic.

With a static IP, the IP address always remains the same. For example, campus printers may use a static IP address so that a computer always knows where to find the printer. When an IoT-managed switch is embedded into a campus's environmental system, perhaps a thermostat or a light switch, the permanent placement can utilize a static address. Once attached to the network, a phone-based app will identify and use the address whenever it controls the embedded object.

However, student devices on campus may utilize a dynamic IP address. A dynamic IP address changes each time the user accesses the network. With a dynamic address, each time the student logs on, works, then logs off, a different IP address within the defined range can be used. This also adds a layer of security.

A school has a defined range of IP addresses available. The addresses may be acquired from the Internet service provider, or the college may purchase its block directly from the American Registry of Internet Numbers (www.ARIN.net), ensuring that they can retain their numbers should they change ISPs.

Now that you know about the unique identifier (IP address) each device is assigned, how does that work with a laptop, mobile phone, tablet, watch, or other device that has no wired connection?

WHAT IS WI-FI AND WHERE DOES IT COME FROM?

Society today has moved to wireless. All computers now routinely come with wireless access. All newer handheld devices are wireless. As you have learned, even household appliances and household control devices are wireless. You may have seen or heard the term *Wi-Fi* (or *WiFi*) to indicate wireless connectivity options for equipment. The term does not actually have a definition but was rather a marketing takeoff created from the 1950s term *HiFi*, which was used for high-fidelity audio recordings when higher-resolution vinyl records became commonplace. Wi-Fi adopted and modified the term when wireless was first becoming common.

When an ISP is selected, that provider specifies the properties for or includes a connection device for the service. This device is normally a modem (modulator/demodulator—converts an analog signal to digital) or a router (a networking device that forwards data packets between the network and the computer) or a combination of the two.

For most homes, the router also provides a wireless signal to the home. This enables multiple devices such as computers, handheld devices (tablets, cell phones, music players), television receivers (such as Apple TV, Amazon Fire TV, Google Chromecast, Roku Player), home automation devices (such as thermostats, garage door openers, security cameras, door locks), home communication devices (such as Amazon Echo, Apple HomePod, or Google Home), and other devices to communicate via the Internet. These are a few examples of the "things" in the Internet of Things.

Although these devices are designed to provide a signal to the entire home, depending on your home, you may need to extend that range. The most recent development is mesh technology. With mesh technology, the user has multiple connection points throughout the building. Each of these connection points communicates with the others, with the main mesh point picking up the signal from the wireless router provided by the ISP. This spreads the wireless signal throughout the home. Examples of mesh systems for the home are Google Wifi, Luma, Orbi, eero, and Linksys Velop.

Campuses and multilevel corporate facilities have been equipped with multiple wireless access points for most of the 21st century. Demand for wireless has placed a heavy load on these access points, and institutions discovered a need to replace the access points every few years. To date, these access points are all wired to the campus or company network.

COPPER AND FIBER

Now, take a quick look at the different delivery methods for providing a connection to the Internet. This was briefly touched on in the previous section of this chapter, but a more in-depth perspective is needed. Basically, a signal reaches your home, school, or business in one of three ways: telephone line (DSL), cable (CATV), or fiber (fiber optic). Here is an overview of those options:[5]

Fiber Optics	• The signal is provided via laser light traveling through a glass fiber. Multiple fiber strands are in a bundle, with a pair required to transmit signals each direction. • Technology has enabled the strands to be subdivided and purchased as individual "waves" of light. The waves can be differentiated via light color (red, blue, green) or by polarization. • Waves are further subdivided by size so that a buyer can purchase bandwidth in amounts (generally created by Ethernet) in 10 Mbps, 100 Mbps, 1 Gbps, 10 Gbps, or 100 Gbps segments.
Coaxial Cable	• The signal is delivered by a bundle of coaxial conductive metal strands. At the core is a copper wire, but it may have various thicknesses. • Whereas a fiber signal may travel several miles without a boost by amplification, cable will need a boost every 1,000 to 1,600 feet according to the thickness of the copper. Cable is able to carry a good bit of capacity with current technologies. Up to 40 Gbps can be reached today, with innovation regularly increasing the top numbers. • Cable is still far more widely deployed and saturates more neighborhoods than fiber.
DSL	• Delivers Internet via a traditional phone line, most frequently with a copper "twisted-pair." • Bandwidth is usually limited to less than 100 Mbps, and the line may be shared with the phone service and other household services from the phone company. DSL will be focused on home applications, small businesses, or remote teaching centers rather than fully operational campuses. • Phone lines are available in a far broader number of locations. However, even phone companies are using fiber for longer-haul applications where their business models justify it.

Realistically, both DSL and cable are considered copper as the method of transmission involves copper wire. Information is transmitted using electrical signals. Distance degradation and magnetic/electrical interference is possible. But as you can see, 90% of the country is covered by DSL, cable, or both.

Fiber delivers information via pulses of light generated by a laser. There is very minimal distance degradation, and interference is nonexistent.

A break in a telephone line or television cable is fairly easy to repair. A break in a fiber-optic cable is much more challenging. However, fiber cables are buried underground, so a weather-related break is unlikely. Fiber also does not depend on electricity for transmission except at the laser end, where the signal is generated.

The capacity of fiber is greater than that of either cable or telephone lines, but for residential use, the transmission speeds of cable and telephone lines reach 100 Mbps or more. Your existing ISP may be able to upgrade your service for only a few additional dollars per month.

And speaking of fiber, you may have heard the term *dark fiber*. What is it, and what is it for? In anticipation of high demand, telecommunications companies laid thousands of miles of fiber-optic cable back in the 1990s. However, the world has gone largely wireless, leaving much of the fiber unused. Unused fiber-optic cable is also known as *unlit* or *dark fiber*.

So what happens to the millions of miles of unused dark fiber? The door is open for global expansion and connection of enterprises, scientific communities, global financial conglomerates, and worldwide educational endeavors. With the connections already in place, institutions large and small have an opportunity to expand global reach without investing in infrastructure. An online search for "using dark fiber" nets over 1.5 million hits. The opportunities are endless.

Now that you understand copper, fiber, and dark fiber, turn your attention to how all of the computers on your campus are connected. Obviously, each computer does not have its own separate connection to the Internet. Entities with multiple computer users utilize a networking technology known as *Ethernet*.

ETHERNET

What is Ethernet, and how is it different from all the other nets?

The term *Ethernet* refers to the networking technology and the transmission of data over a wired network within a defined space (such as your building on campus). It is not only the equipment but the method of transmission that allows information to get from your computer to another computer without any loss.

Your office computer on campus is probably connected to the network using a colored cable (green, blue, yellow, or any of many other colors) between the computer and an outlet in the wall that appears to be similar to the telephone connection. Somewhere in the building is a network closet within which is what is called a *switch*. Switches are covered in the next section, but if you were to see this switch, you would see many flashing lights (indicating network activity) and various colored cables. Each of those cables goes to a computer or a programmable device. Your campus includes many of these network closets. The cables are called *Ethernet cables*, and they link the computers to the main campus network through the switch.

HUBS, SWITCHES, AND ROUTERS

If you set up your own home wireless network, you may have heard the terms *hub*, *switch*, and *router*. Even if you have never installed your own home network, you have likely heard your college IT (information technology) technician refer to the devices' names. Here are some details about each of the devices and what they do. Some of the devices are "intelligent," with an embedded capability to learn things, but for the most part they perform similar tasks.

Hub—A hub is the least costly, least complicated, and least intelligent of the three devices. It has one job, connecting computers. Information coming from one computer is distributed to all computers connected to the hub. Responses are also sent to all computers. It is similar to the old "party line" telephones, where everyone could hear everyone. If you do not know what a party line is, ask your grandparents and plan for a few surprising stories.

Switch—A switch is a more efficient hub. It, too, connects computers. But instead of automatically routing information to all computers, it "learns" where information comes from and goes to, and when responses come back, it routes those responses only to the original sender. So using the party-line analogy (did you ask your grandparents yet?), instead of a phone call ringing all phones, the phone call only goes to one phone. It is essential for businesses and educational institutions to use a switch instead of a hub.

Router—A router is an intelligent device. Routers can be programmed to understand, manipulate, and route data. A router is essentially a computer designed to handle network traffic. Routers are used in major network hubs (such as your ISP) to help handle the monumental amount of traffic clogging the Internet today.

Many people refer to these three devices as if they were one in the same, but the expectations, capabilities, and cost differences dictate a clear distinction between the three. Your home network device is probably *not* a router. The little wireless hub you can purchase at a retailer for a few dollars is definitely not a router.

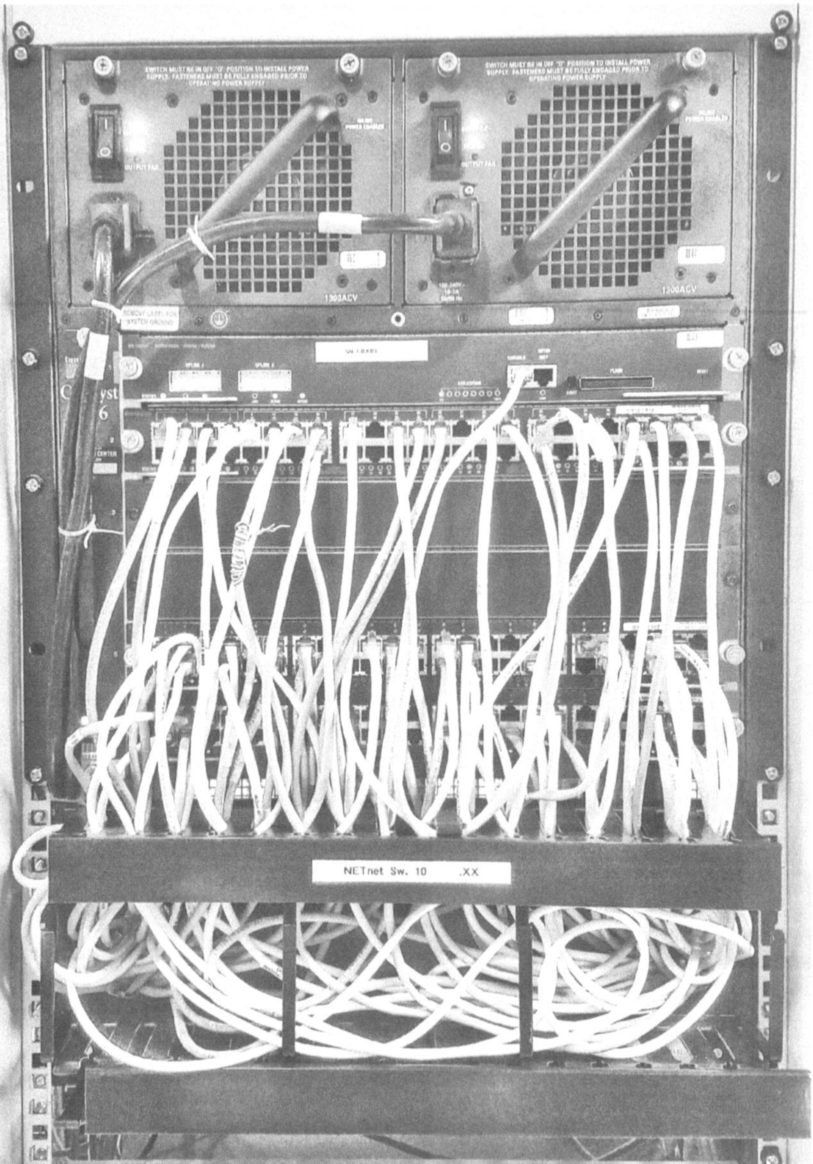

Figure 6.4. Cable rack with switches. ***Courtesy of Mickey Slimp***

WHERE DOES "THE CLOUD" COME IN?

Cloud computing, essentially connecting through the Internet to a remote server and/or application, is much more prevalent than most people believe. Without realizing it, almost everyone with a cell phone uses cloud computing on a monthly, weekly, daily, or even hourly basis.

For many, hearing the term *in the cloud* engenders a mysterious and almost mystical vision of technology simultaneously wonderful and beyond reach. In effect, it has much in common with the Wizard of Oz. Like the Wizard, once you strip away the magical marketing hype, there is actually something solid there that can be quite useful.

Here is a look at the types of third-party applications that are based on cloud computing. You simply access a server through an Internet connection and you are on your way.

- Email services: Gmail, Yahoo Mail, Outlook, smartphone-related mail, or any online email service
- Chat and instant messaging services too numerous to mention
- Social networking: Twitter, Facebook, Snapchat, Instagram, LinkedIn, and many others. As new "hot" social networking applications emerge, others wane or disappear.
- Hosted application services, such as Google Docs
- File-sharing services, such as Dropbox

Where a lot of people falter is in not realizing the potential for and the immediacy of a widespread distribution of anything entered into a cloud application. An ill-stated tweet can cost a job or a reputation. A funny chat might be screen shot and posted on an individual site, only to be reposted on hundreds of others. Your Facebook "check-in" tells the world you're somewhere else—perhaps even thousands of miles away from your home.

Cloud computing combined with today's immediate technologies requires more than an awareness of the implications of information. As an educator enters information into the web-based universe, the potential impact the information can have on both yourself and others has to be kept in mind.

TYPES OF CLOUDS

Just as atmospheric clouds come in several varieties—stratus, cirrus, and cumulus—the clouds providing network support do the same. The most common forms, as described by Arron Fu of Uniprint.net[6] are private, community, and public clouds. Networking clouds can also take a hybrid form, mixing the characteristics of the other models.

Private Clouds—In education, a private cloud can offer an off-site server to provide specific software to a campus. The external server might be at the administrative center for a multicampus institution, at a server farm connected by a direct fiber line or by a virtual private network (VPN) built within an Ethernet or Internet connection, or at a software vendor's computing center as a virtual server dedicated to the college. A firewall would protect entry in and out of the cloud-based services and other security measures to ensure a level of security equal to that of a local area network (LAN) on campus would be in place.

Private cloud networks are just as often acquired to provide a college with access to specialized personnel or software skills available at the contracted server site. A smaller college using an Oracle-based financial management software might have difficulty acquiring a $100,000-plus certified software specialist on their own. As the work by the specialist is only needed at limited times, it makes sense to contract with a focused, cloud-based group that can offer the service.

Now that a number of independent servers can be virtualized and placed on remote boxes, it may also make sense to provide their maintenance off-site, again sharing the costs of personnel and hardware with other unaffiliated users. Rates for the service may run by the hour or be contracted as a monthly or annual service.

Public Cloud—When exploring the concept of a public cloud, think Facebook or maybe a number of the other apps that are housed on your phone. You basically trade control of the networking for free or inexpensive access. Generally, you also trade off some level of access to your personal data, either for marketing purposes, general analytic research, or to allow others to direct information your way.

Many of the controlling apps for IoT devices, particularly for personal use or for the home, are delivered through a public cloud. The free connection is provided to ensure your ability to use and enjoy the product. You, of course, provide an email and the analytics collected directly from the device that can be used to upgrade the service and to offer you related devices in the future. The cost is normally free but can take the form of a monthly license or a pay-by-use fee.

Community Clouds—Community clouds are normally provided among entities or industries with a common purpose yet still require much the same level of security as a private cloud. Library database services in Texas are offered through TexShare, a community cloud resourced through state funds and some user fees. All schools can connect, yet specific protocols control the access.

A shared ERP (enterprise resource program) at the state level is a similar use for a community cloud, as would be a centralized commercial service maintaining medical records. The records might only be available to a university health science center and its related clinics but would be accessible from any of those locations.

EQUIPMENT AND SOFTWARE: PLANNING FOR UPGRADES AND OBSOLESCENCE

A bane of every college's information technology efforts has been the ongoing costs of maintenance and hardware. Between planned obsolescence, end-of-life announcements from vendors, and annual software license requirements, maintaining a stable and reasonable budget requires a herculean effort.

During the first decade of the 21st century, the biggest upgrade worry was with the hardware itself. Schools adopted regularly scheduled replacement of computer lab and office computers, the thought being that the equipment somehow "wore out" after a certain number of years. At the same time, higher-end equipment from the technology divisions—that is, the teaching programs such as drafting, engineering, networking technology, or gaming—would be repurposed after four years, using one department's "worn out" equipment to replace even older office equipment in the library.

The biggest upgrade reason in the second decade of the century and beyond is likewise capacity based but focuses more on personal devices than computers. The smartphone in your pocket has significantly more capacity than the personal computer of 15 years ago. Consumers expect instantaneous gratification, and older personal devices do not have the capacity to deliver the current expectations created by the growth of apps and IoT.

What was once a four- to six- and then a three- to five-year cycle of obsolescence is now, realistically, only one to two years. While consumers enjoy the battle of manufacturers trying to outdo each other with the latest and greatest Android or iPhone, the bandwidth demands of the newer products simply add to the strain on what is likely an already overburdened network.

A new student on campus may own between three and five devices that need a network connection. At a small school where 300 students live on site, that creates a possibility of 1,500 new devices.

What are those devices? Laptops. Smartphones. Tablets. Gaming consoles. Home voice assistants like Apple HomePod or Amazon Echo. Network-based TV receivers. Smart watches. "Find me" key fobs. Speakers. And any number of new products being released almost daily.

That new one gigabit network the technology department so proudly introduced could be struggling in a year and completely outdated in two.

SERVER CAPACITY

Most of the larger applications used by colleges are housed on servers. Servers are generally larger computers or processor-containing boxes with enough memory and storage to hold the software needed for a process. Common larger applications needing server support include the campus enterprise resource program or ERP, composed of a student information system, the personnel and human resources file, payroll, the purchasing software, and similar routines. Other server-based applications could include the learning management system (LMS) for online courses, the library catalog system, or the college website.

Two decades ago, server capacity was relatively easy to determine. Servers were locally based on campus and were usually designed to handle a single task or several related tasks. For example, a college could have a server for email, a server for library databases, a server for the campus website, and so forth.

Campus-based servers cost anywhere from a few thousand dollars to tens of thousands, needed periodic upgrading, and almost always needed additional storage capacity, with a longer life that meant replacement on an eight-year cycle was warranted. Today's applications include far more graphics and web pages than simple text, so programs require a hundred times the storage or more than just a few years ago.

Most computer centers today employ virtual servers, however, deflecting or eliminating the need for costly on-campus equipment and upkeep. But planning for the right capacity is more challenging because virtual servers perform more than one task and can house multiple applications.

Resource planning has become critical. Too many resources mean paying for unused capacity, which few colleges can afford. Too few resources can cripple an organization. Slow applications can lead to grumbling throughout the institution and has led to more than one CIO's departure.

Capacity planning now relies on IoT and related software tools that monitor and track resource usage over time. With embedded analytics to predict future capacity needs, the tools generate alarms when resource shortages occur.

In the recent past, the tools were only as good as the IT management team's attention span and their ability to influence their leadership. When the IT group failed to pay attention to growing resource demands, system performance degraded. In worst-case scenarios, the server became unstable or even crashed.[7]

Constructed within the overall business and change plan for the institution, however, IoT-based tools can be accessed throughout the decision chain, making a need for server space, greater network speeds, and alternate access routes obvious. Where the technology most helps is in providing you and your team an accurate assessment before the crisis hits.

NOTES

1. *Oxford English Dictionary*. 2018. "Internet." Retrieved from https://en.oxforddictionaries.com/definition/internet.
2. Rousseau, James Jacques. 2004. *Emile*. Urbana, IL; Project Gutenberg. Retrieved May 28, 2018, from http://www.gutenberg.org/ebooks/5427.
3. Clemson University. 2018. "Wide-Area-Networking." Clemson Computing and Information Technology (CCIT). Accessed May 29, 2018. Retrieved from https://ccit.clemson.edu/services/network-phones-cable/network/wide-area-networking/.
4. Donnigan, Mark. 2016. "Immersive VR and 360 Video at Streamable Bitrates: Are You Crazy?" *BEAMR Blog*. Accessed May 29, 2018. Retrieved from http://blog.beamr.com/2016/10/28/immersive-vr-and-360-video-at-streamable-bitrates-are-you-crazy/.
5. Cooper, Tyler. 2018. "DSL vs Cable vs Fiber: Comparing Internet Options." BroadbandNow. Accessed January 23, 2018. Retrieved from https://broadbandnow.com/report/dsl-vs-cable-vs-fiber/.
6. Fu, Arron. 2017. "7 Different Types of Cloud Computing Structures." UniPrint. Accessed June 3, 2018. Retrieved from https://www.uniprint.net/en/7-types-cloud-computing-structures/.
7. Bigelow, Stephen J. 2014. "Why Is Virtual Server Capacity Planning So Difficult?" *Essential Guide: Develop a Solid Virtualization Capacity Planning*. TechTarget, January 2014. Retrieved from http://searchservervirtualization.techtarget.com/feature/Why-is-virtual-server-capacity-planning-so-difficult.

Chapter Seven

College Facilities in the Digital Age

The campus network offers a vital piece of infrastructure that takes a much higher priority within the digital age. Nonetheless, that does not mean campuses, facilities, and facility-driven processes are disappearing. Yet in the world of the Internet of Things (IoT), it is time to review each building, each structure, and each process to determine how it can work better and where IoT can make life both simpler and richer for the student.

EMBEDDED TECHNOLOGY THROUGHOUT THE ORGANIZATION

The idea behind the Internet of Things is that through the embedding of technology into physical units, processes can be improved. Generally, embedded technology is not generated by a fully functional computer. Rather, a processing device serving as a "dedicated computer system designed for one or two specific functions"[1] is put into place.

An example would be a motion-detecting lighting controller. Specially designed sensors within the device detect motion to trigger the on-and-off function. Connectivity to an external computing network provides a function for timed lighting while also collecting and maintaining records of the on-and-off function.

For resource utilization, an Internet-driven washing machine could detect the presence of a load of clothing. Advanced sensors could identify color densities and, by weight and volume, a general sense of fabric, which could be overridden by local control. Connection to a network could interface the IoT device with the utility company schedules. As a result, the wash is timed to coincide with the lowest cost-time interval for electricity during the day or night.

Embedded technology can be considered to include many of the limited-purpose components of a networking system, such as routers, bridges, and switches, running into costs of tens to hundreds of thousands of dollars. Once the systemic components are in place, however, most embedded items are simply parts or plug-ins to control discrete tasks within a larger product or system.

Embedded systems and embedded components with a limited number of computing functions are built into a large number of devices in daily use. More complicated types of apparatus include automated teller machines

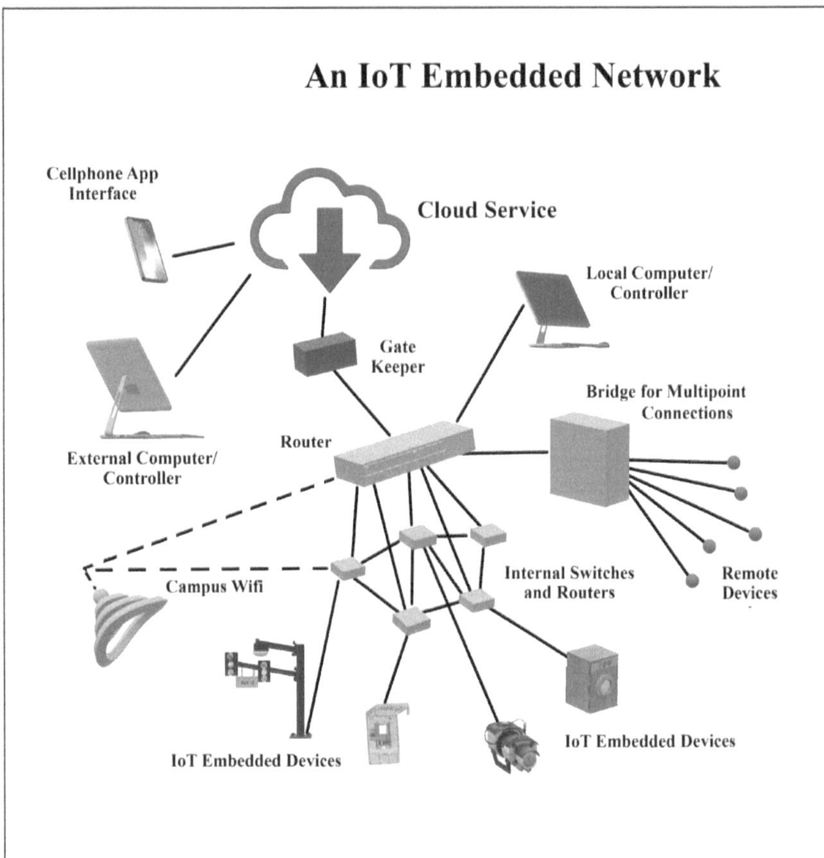

Figure 7.1. *Courtesy of Roy Bartels and Mickey Slimp*

(ATMs), cell phones, calculators, video game consoles, multifunction printers, and thermostats.

Handheld computers or tablets may also be considered embedded devices because of the nature of their hardware design, even though they are more expandable in software terms. This line of definition between embedded devices and full computers will continue to blur as computer memory chips become smaller, cheaper, and easier to place in every device.

RETHINKING CAMPUS FACILITIES

So as new facilities are put into place, older facilities are upgraded, or as functions are simply reviewed to improve service and student outcomes, how can Internet-driven technologies improve the college's operations? In nearly every area of the campus, new efficiencies are waiting to be discovered. With monitoring and sensory tools that seemed miraculous at the turn of the century, IoT is remaking the possibilities for the campus infrastructure.

ENERGY EFFICIENCY

Energy efficiency emerged in the last decades of the 20th century as power consumption strained power grids. Motion-sensing light switches have been around since the 1960s, but what was once a fascinating gadget soon worked its way into buildings, with rooms that sensed movement and used that sense to determine if the lights should be on or off.

The same power-saving opportunity is still available today, but now entire buildings can be controlled through a simple panel in a single office. Or in the case of your home, an app on your smartphone can turn lights on and off automatically, raise and lower the thermostat, unlock the door or open the garage, or water the yard.

For a number of years, motion-sensing water faucets, toilets, and soap dispensers have been in place in public facilities. By connecting the embedded sensors under centralized control, settings allow for timing the availability of hot water, monitoring for leaks and stresses, automating cutoffs in case of emergencies, and rerouting waterflow for high-use periods. A continuous, excess water flow in a restroom could trigger an alert to either maintenance or security while maintaining a timed record in case of vandalism to coincide with entryway security cameras.

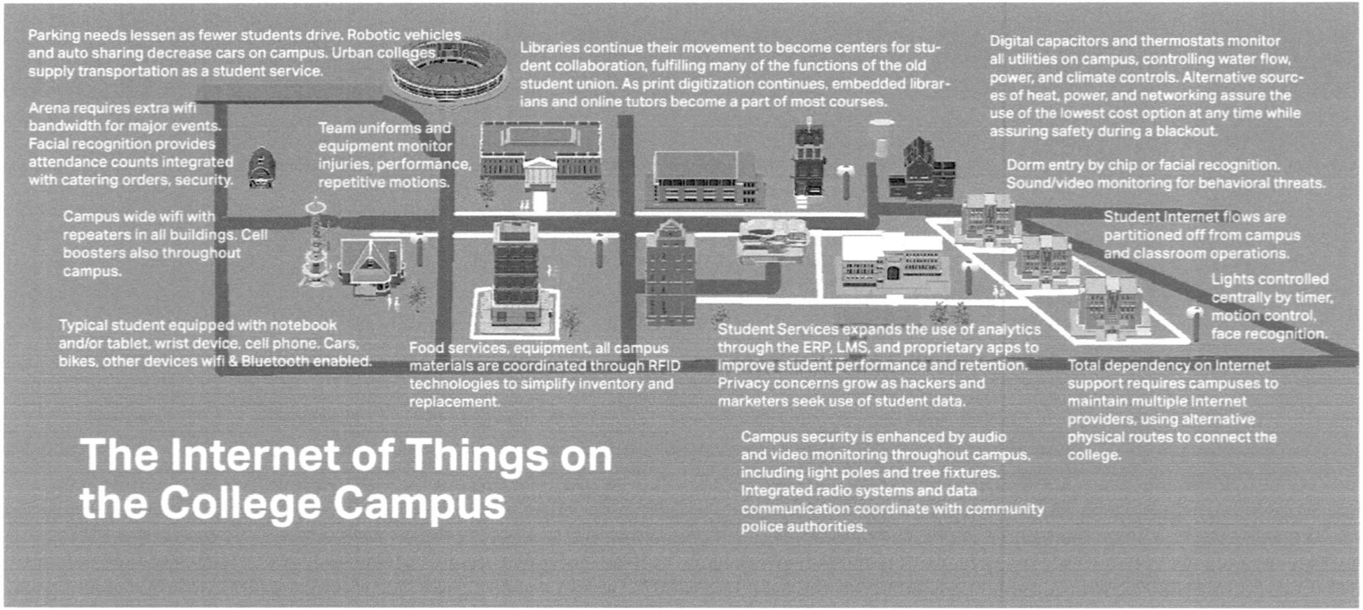

Figure 7.2. *Courtesy of Kevin and Mickey Slimp*

INVENTORY MANAGEMENT

Campuses have a tremendous amount of capital tied up in equipment. Expensive equipment—how is it tracked? Not just location but hours of usage, repairs, applications added, peripherals attached, and age?

When a faculty member changes an office and takes a computer or even a bookshelf along, how is the equipment's relocation tracked? Many schools still use spreadsheets to track inventory. So when a particular computer is logged to be in Room 5102 and the faculty member moves to Room 8110, who updates the spreadsheet?

Using a spreadsheet or another manual process makes it nearly impossible to accurately and consistently track location, value, or condition. People make mistakes. Whether it is a simple keystroke error, an oversight, or something else, slipups happen.

Some users on a campus will require more robust equipment than others. A clerk who simply accesses text-based data does not need the latest processor, an extensive amount of computer memory, or a high-end graphics card. A marketing department employee, a webmaster, or a geophysics instructor will need equipment that can handle the demands of the job. How are those differences tracked?

In the first chapter of this book, radio-frequency identification (RFID) was introduced as the barcoding technology that started the whole Internet of Things adventure. By the second chapter, Johnny had mastered IoT technology sufficiently to troubleshoot a problem at his workplace. Savvy campuses are adopting RFID to help track all aspects of their inventory.

When a piece of equipment is received, it is tagged and entered into the system with information regarding its brand, model, and serial number; its processor, memory, and RAM capacity; and other specifications. As software is installed (Microsoft Windows or Adobe Creative Cloud, for example), the information goes in the database, tagged to that particular piece of equipment. Once the machine is installed in a location, that office or classroom is added to the database and so it is integrated into the RFID chip.

Any required maintenance for each piece of equipment is logged at the time service is performed, with the next maintenance automatically scheduled. Any repairs are logged as they are accomplished. So when the next problem is reported, the help team can pull up the specifications, location, and history of any unit in just seconds.

How is location determined? In Chapter 2, you witnessed Johnny narrowing down the location of a problem. Watch as Johnny tackles another issue.

Johnny is growing a lot from his internship in efficiency management. As he entered Marble Worldwide Delivery today, his presence is logged and his workstation is activated. He takes a seat at his terminal and nods to Fred, his supervisor.

"Anything new today?"

His mentor eyes him. "You always seem to get here early. When I was your age, I strolled in everywhere at least five minutes late. I assume you have big plans for tonight. I'm envious."

Johnny grins.

"How does anyone survive these days to be forty," Fred chuckles but knows that Johnny's generation takes their work more seriously than his ever did.

"We had five expensive Internet filtering devices ship out of here two days ago. Verify they were delivered yesterday."

"Any specifics?" Johnny asks.

"They are $25,000 apiece. Is that enough?"

Johnny nods and speaks to his terminal. "Show shipments from two days ago. Equipment cost: $25,000."

"I'll check for you, Johnny," the terminal responds. Seconds later, five shipping manifests appear on the screen. "I show we shipped five units matching that price range two days ago."

Johnny likes the kind, female voice from his terminal. He scans the list.

The first item shows delivery confirmed to a community college in Illinois yesterday.

The second item shows delivery confirmed to a community college in Oregon yesterday.

The third item shows on hold.

The fourth item shows delivery confirmed to a community college in Texas yesterday.

The fifth item shows in-transit with an expected delivery to a community college in South Carolina later today.

Johnny speaks to his terminal. "Status of item 3?"

"I'll check," the terminal responds. "Truck is offline. Observation drone shows truck is undergoing repairs. Checking for status."

Johnny waits.

"Fuel cell problem. The repair drone states that repairs are near completion."

"Notify customer of the delay, and report to me when the truck is underway. Customer may contact me with any questions."

"Yes, Johnny."

"Status of item 5. Reason for delay?"

"I'll check," the terminal responds. "Observation drone shows large boulder on highway. Traffic rerouting caused delay. Shipment is now underway. Delivery expected momentarily."

"Notify customer. Customer may contact me with any questions."

Some of Johnny's experience is already available today. A shipping status report with daily progress is common. Yet between major checkpoints, no one knows exactly where the merchandise is. Reports mostly indicate a time and date the item left one facility and arrived at another. And if delays occur, the arrival time is simply extended. Still, only a very small percentage of shipments arrive the next day instead of the promised delivery day.

As you saw with Johnny's example, hyper-GPS boosts location accuracy to a few millimeters instead of 10 feet. Multipoint connections with driverless vehicles means no loss of vehicle guidance and constant communication between the vehicle and checkpoints. Observation drones not only provide visual confirmation but an additional connection point.

The customer order in the system triggers robotic warehouse retrieval. As the item is loaded in the truck bound for the delivery area, the truck is scanned to confirm item receipt and the customer information is automatically loaded in the truck database. Truck location and status is always known, and drones capture visuals. But the information is stored until requested. As you can tell by Johnny's communication with his terminal, requests are fulfilled within seconds.

Why is this important to a college campus? When a piece of equipment is moved, sensors can track the time and date it was removed from one location and the time and date it arrived in another. Through the use of RFID in student ID cards and campus employee badges, the person who moved the device is also known.

If you are thinking about a desktop computer, refocus your thoughts onto notebooks, tablets, and other handheld devices. RFID can track the movement of anything that is tagged. And just as groceries come from the manufacturer with barcodes in place, equipment manufacturers are starting to place built-in RFID chips and location software into their equipment. In a situation where classrooms are stocked with handheld devices (for example, high-end graphing calculators or iPads), tracking when one of those expensive devices leaves the classroom and who carried it is important.

Inventory control built on chips and sensors is available today. Price tags and in-house expertise may have slowed its deployment on some campuses. Still, well before 2030, completely automated inventory controls using RFID will be the standard.

HUMAN TRAFFIC AND CROWD CONTROL

Between class periods, where is the busiest place on campus? You probably know that from simple observation or listening to students complain. Not only do the crowds in the hallway or on the campus "quad" irritate students rushing from class to class, they can present a security nightmare. One punch is thrown and many students could be hurt. Local gangs bringing turf issues or recruiting on campus? Gunfire? You get the picture.

So how do you know exactly how many students are coming or going throughout the campus? Just as with the material elements, crowd management can use RFID technology with chips embedded into student and faculty IDs. With IoT embedded sensors throughout the campus, network software can track each student passing by or near a chip-sensing device.

Face recognition software using chips and cameras embedded directly into the campus routers and switches also offers a rapid recognition and response record of who is or is not onsite. Facial recognition tools now have the ability to keep class attendance and potentially to even monitor student attentiveness. As the software can be integrated into student data records or juxtaposed alongside external police databases, it creates obvious concerns related to FERPA (the Family Educational Rights and Privacy Act), raising privacy and records management issues.

SCHEDULING

Course scheduling, particularly for on-campus classes, will always be a challenge. Most scheduling is predictive. Scheduling is based on course enrollment data over a period of years. The course schedule for fall is likely based on enrollment in courses the previous fall and spring.

The availability of facilities and faculty also has an impact. Students all want 9:00 a.m. and 10:00 a.m. classes so they can sleep late and be out of class in time for lunch. Yet core courses or classes by popular teachers with the highest enrollment often need to be spread throughout the day.

Course schedules are planned two or three years in advance. For two-year schools, this essentially allows the student to plan the schedule for his or her entire college enrollment period. This also allows the college to predict what is needed in the future and gear instructor load based on that prediction. If additional faculty are needed, that need is established well in advance, giving the college time to recruit, hire, and train the new teachers.

IoT-generated analytics are likewise playing a role in the scheduling process. The analytics provided by the various data-centric predictive foot-traffic monitoring tools such as ID chips and facial recognition can be integrated into the student information system to help with scheduling. Knowing how many students are going to which classes at what time can offer schedule variations to turn logjams into a smoother flow of pedestrians, easing congestion, frustrations, and flare-ups.

When it comes to facilities (on-campus classrooms), this same scheduling idea can apply. Course enrollment history provides data listing the highest enrollment courses. So instead of scheduling four English 101 courses in the humanities building at 9:00 a.m., those courses can be spread out throughout the day, eliminating the logjam of students rushing to/from and into/out of the building.

Take a look at a case study done by Tarrant County College District. It highlights challenges with Wi-Fi capacity, tracking personnel and equipment using RFID technology.

CASE STUDY: TARRANT COUNTY COLLEGE DISTRICT WIRELESS NETWORKS: MORE THAN JUST A GATEWAY TO THE INTERNET

By Richard Sullivan

With the explosion of wireless devices, especially across the higher education environment, having a wireless network that is robust and responsive enough for today's student is imperative. In 2012, Tarrant County College District (TCCD), located in and around the Fort Worth, Texas, metro area, had fewer than 100 wireless access points (WAP) across its five physical campuses. Providing wireless connectivity for over 50,000[a] undergraduate students, TCCD knew it had to change in order to meet the expectations of its faculty, students, parents, and the local community. As of this writing, TCCD has over 1,000 WAPs across its campuses and continues to expand and innovate its wireless access technology.

In February of 2016, Cisco made the following six predictions:[b]

1. Global mobile data traffic will increase 8X
2. About 70% of the world's population (7.8 billion people) will be mobile users
3. There will be approximately 11.6 mobile-ready devices/connections
4. Mobile video will represent 75% of global mobile data traffic

(continued)

5. Smartphones, laptops, and tablets will drive about 92% of global mobile
6. By 2015, there were nearly 96 million wearable devices in use. By 2020, there will be more than 600 million wearable devices in use.

With the innovations coming from Apple, Samsung, and other wireless manufacturers, Cisco may have underestimated the number of wearable devices. Likewise, with services from Netflix, YouTube, and other streaming media providers, TCCD is seeing a tremendous increase in demand on bandwidth and especially on the wireless network.

The Pew Research Center reports,

> Many American households have multiple devices—especially smartphones. A third of American households have three or more smartphones, compared with 23% that have three or more desktops, 17% that have three or more tablets and only 7% that have three or more streaming media devices.
>
> Taken together, 90% of U.S. households contain at least one of these devices (smartphone, desktop/laptop computer, tablet or streaming media device), with the typical (median) American household containing five of them. And nearly one-in-five American households (18%) are "hyper-connected"—meaning they contain 10 or more of these devices.[c]

Going back to 2012 again, all of TCCD's Internet traffic ran through a single connection point at 400 Mbps. Looking at feedback from students and faculty, the bandwidth was increased to 800 Mbps and immediately upgraded to 1 Gbps following an iOS release by Apple that saw everyone with an Apple product downloading their upgrade on the TCCD network. This large and unforeseen event almost shut down all other Internet connections.

In 2013, TCCD purchased direct Internet access for each of the four other physical campuses, created a private network for faculty and staff, and created a public network for students and the community to use. In 2018, TCCD is again looking to increase Internet bandwidth to keep up with the demands created primarily by mobile wireless devices.

BEYOND BYOD

While this is good for the current user community, TCCD wanted the wireless network to do more than just provide Internet or academic access. Looking at several areas where the wireless network could be expanded beyond its base use, TCCD is focusing on business needs as well as student needs beyond the academic. If your environment is similar to TCCD's, your asset management team spends a tremendous number of hours hunting, documenting, and tracking assets. With asset management in mind,

1. What if your assets could be queried and update a database with their current location?
2. What if reports on your assets provided updates on unplanned or unauthorized movements of these assets?

With the refinements in radio-frequency identification or RFID, Wi-Fi-based and Bluetooth-enabled tags supporting real-time location systems (RTLS), TCCD has begun investigating as to how best to use the wireless network to collect and report asset data. In order to collect the data, the wireless network has to be capable of collecting and reporting on the asset's location.

TCCD's wireless network, built on Cisco WAPs, is currently undergoing an upgrade to access points that support the Cisco Hyperlocation[d] tool set. The plan is to work with RFID, Bluetooth Low Energy (BLE), and Wi-Fi-based RTLS tag providers to determine which combination works best with the hyperlocation application.

Note: While TCCD is working on solutions using Cisco-based products, other network and electronic manufacturing companies have similar technologies that could offer a solution for your environment.

Figure 7.3. ***Courtesy of Cisco Networks***

SAFETY AND SECURITY

While tracking inanimate objects is important, our most important asset is our students. At TCCD, we have a three-week summer program for students from third grade to eighth grade called College for Kids. TCCD believes that using hyperlocation services and beaconing wristbands or the student's smartphone, staff can better track the movement of these students, providing an improved level of safety and security.

For all of TCCD's students, faculty, staff, and community users, by being better in

- identifying our students and what technologies are being used on the campuses and

(continued)

- determining where the students congregate and what their travel patterns are

TCCD can begin to

- deliver better geolocation services for the students to find their way around the campuses and
- deliver timely information for activities close to the student's current location.

By providing an environment in which faculty, staff, students, and the local community can receive timely and important updates to activities or issues on the various campuses, TCCD will not only improve the experiences of our students, faculty, staff, and the community but also improve on the security and safety of our campuses.

Richard Sullivan is the chief information officer for the Tarrant County College District in Fort Worth, Texas. He holds a master of network and communication degree from the Keller Graduate School of Management. In the past, he has held positions at SunGard Higher Education and at Electronic Data Systems (EDS).

NOTES

a. Office of Institutional Research, Tarrant County College. 2017. "Table 2: 2017FL Headcount, Enrolments, Contact Hours, and Semester Hours." In *Statistical Handbook FL 2017*, p. 5. Fort Worth, TX: Tarrant County College. Retrieved from https://www.tccd.edu/documents/about/research/institutional-intelligence-and-research/statistical-handbook/2017FL-statistical-handbook.pdf.

b. Chan, Stephanie. 2016. "6 Mobility Predictions for 2020." The Network: Cisco's Technology News Site, February 3, 2016. Retrieved from https://newsroom.cisco.com/feature-content?type=webcontent&articleId=1741578. Used with the permission of The Network: Cisco's Technology News Site (https://thenetwork.cisco.com/).

c. Olmstead, Kenneth. 2017. "A Third of Americans Live in a Household with Three or More Smartphones." Fact Tank—Our Lives in Numbers, Pew Research Center, May 25, 2017. Retrieved from http://www.pewresearch.org/fact-tank/2017/05/25/a-third-of-americans-live-in-a-household-with-three-or-more-smartphones/.

d. Cisco. 2018. "Cisco® Hyperlocation Module with Advanced Security." Accessed June 5, 2018. Retrieved from https://www.cisco.com/c/en/us/support/interfaces-modules/aironet-hyperlocation-module-advanced-security/model.html?dtid=osscdc000283.

CAR TRAFFIC ON CAMPUS

Considering most end-of-the-year student evaluations, on-campus parking nearly always is at or near the top of the student complaint list. There are two sides to the issue. On one hand, if parking is an issue, it is an indicator of growth and thus an issue to be dealt with but not an insurmountable problem. On the other hand, many campuses are landlocked, so parking only comes through the construction of a parking facility. That means a single space can add up to tens of thousands of dollars or even more than $100,000 in construction costs.

The Internet of Things should ease the parking issue for urban campuses within the coming decade. Many millennial and Generation Z students are already delaying the acquisition of a first driver's license, using public transportation, bicycling, or ride sharing to get around. With the advent of self-driving vehicles, ride sharing should be far more prevalent, while student ownership of a personal vehicle will be in decline.

Uber- and Lyft-type services using self-driving cars will also gain prominence over the next decade, either on a fee-per-ride basis, as is common today, or offering unlimited rides within a given zone based on a monthly rate. Car dealerships or manufacturers could even go the same direction, offering a leased ride service in lieu of today's car lease.

Student tracking and class scheduling software could likewise provide analytical support, supplying information to lay out the number and times cars are needed in advance and in what areas. Markers could even identify students who are running late so that an on-campus shuttle could meet them on their arrival to campus to shorten their time to class.

Where do the vehicles go when not in use? The preferred option would be picking up and transporting another rider. Yet schools will want to maintain some parking nearby so that several cars could always be in the queue. The strategies and rules for vehicle sharing are, nonetheless, still a work in progress. By 2025, however, emerging rules should be much more apparent.

Less urban campuses will see a greater continuing need for personal vehicles, although vehicle management strategies will change. With robotic controls, a personal vehicle can drop a passenger off near his or her destination, then self-drive to a parking area away from the student area. Pickup would only be a few minutes and a phone app away.

Overall, what does all of this mean for parking lots and campus planning? First of all, if the return on investment for a parking facility is greater than seven years, you will want to closely investigate alternatives before committing to a new facility.

Next, consider your options for making the campus more walkable. How protected are campus pedestrians from bad weather? Are shared bikes on campus, released and managed through the student ID, an option? Can shuttles, trolleys, or transports be placed within the campus grounds to facilitate movement? Robotics will come into play here too.

Before funding a new parking facility, also consider an investment in traffic and transportation engineering. As an emerging field of the IoT age, an onsite or contracted traffic engineer can review traffic patterns and data, directing options to best manage the campus flow.

It will likely be well into the 2030s before airborne robotic cars are regular features on a college campus. Yet they will only accelerate the move toward a limited or no on-campus parking scenario. One has to wonder what will replace parking on the list of student complaints.

LABORATORIES AND THE SCIENCES

Until recently, science labs remained specifically hands-on. Courses including lab sessions were only taken on campus. But with the emergence of lower-cost animations, 3-D serious game scenarios, video streaming, and multiuser two-way video, many of the labs can be taken in a virtual setting or as distance courses where lab kits provide the needed tools and accessories.

Video capture enables students, whether on campus or online, to revisit lab experiments as many times as needed. Video of the instructor performing an experiment can be immediately available for students.

With streaming video, students no longer need to crowd around a lab table to watch the instructor dissect that baby pig. They can watch the dissection in high-definition or pull up the streaming video on their smartphone or tablet right there in the lab.

In a multiverse gaming environment, students can relive famous experiments, working alongside discoverers such as Madame Curie or Nikola Tesla. Through gaming or video streams, they can enter some of the world's deepest mines or observe live experiments occurring in earth orbit. Sessions can be scheduled online so that students actually have a brief period to observe planets by remotely controlling the telescopes at a variety of observatories.[2]

ATHLETICS AND IOT

Technology has been a boon to athletics, from the professional level to preschool T-ball games. Even community colleges have seen an uptick in sports, as a drive toward on-campus experiences and community engagement push schools to invest in everything from full-fledged football teams to low-cost frisbee golf and virtual gaming feats. And as sports move from "just for fun" to impacting the college's reputation and recruitment, technology jumps in.

The love of technology began as coaches first gathered their teams for a postgame performance review using home-quality film. A second camera was soon added to the mix, with a focus on individual players. Next, coaches began placing their films in a repository so that teams could share their movies in preparation for meeting their next opposing team. Film gave way to videotape and then to digital recordings. Now combined with online player statistics, an entire suite of sports analytics added complications yet became vital to the players.

Parents and alumni joined the fold, now able to watch their offspring or students online and keep up with the details through live large-screen scoreboards, arena displays, and live feeds via the Internet. Next, as the technology becomes cheaper and more pervasive, college games will continue to follow pro sports in their use of embedded technical tools and analytics.

While games such as baseball have long been deep into statistics, the statistical revolution has become automated and spread across almost all sports. Soccer's English Premier League (EPL) monitors performance in real time via data trackers built into their players' uniforms. With an on-the-field tablet, coaches can tally the information; predict a host of aspects, including a player's chance of injury; compare a team's long-term performance to projected performance in the next game; or decide on the best available player to perform in a given situation. By 2017, nineteen of twenty EPL teams were using analytics software. Each team hosts its own data scientists and performance analysts, looking for correlations and conclusions regarding player performance, match-turning events, and season-wide trends.

Similarly, the National Football League is using "big data" analytics. Sensors in the form of chips inside players' uniforms give viewers and coaches a deeper insight into the players' motions and performance. IoT-based analytics, as a result, are changing both the nature of the statistics and the games themselves.[3]

SOCIAL SPACES FOR LEARNING

Only a few years ago, the imminent death of the school library was widely predicted. Yet as you enter most campuses today, the library is an extremely active place, with private study rooms, student areas for group study and congregation, coffee bars, and high-speed wireless networks. Somewhere around 2010, millennials discovered the library and engendered its conversion into an active social space.

The move to an online environment and virtual engagement has been paralleled by a desire for a planned space for interpersonal contact. Gen Z

Figure 7.4. Social space in the Muntz Library at the University of Texas at Tyler. ***Courtesy of Mickey Slimp***

students and millennials still study in groups, although it seems everyone in the cohort will simultaneously be connected and communicating online. Maintaining a social space for facility planning in the IoT age will continue to be a requirement.

PUBLIC INFORMATION AND MESSAGE CONTROL

Information is at the core of the college mission today. Yet controlling your college's message when you are competing with every person who has a device and can create "truth" is quite the challenge. Take a college campus (or campus system):

- College marketing wants data and information it can share to promote the college. It gets that information from a variety of sources on campus, not just one source (unless, of course, the college president dictates otherwise).
- Financial aid has specific requirements from federal, state, and perhaps local agencies. It must get its information from each of those sources, not just one source.
- Counseling/advising has specific requirements not only for positions within the department but for how students are counseled. They must get their information from a variety of agencies, not just one.
- The college library must provide the same services to distance-learning students as those available to on-campus students. They must get that information from a variety of sources, not just one.
- Add to this student-generated sites from Rate My Professor to Facebook, all creating unique messages and information from the view of an individual student.

Now look at another example totally unrelated to colleges. Suppose you wanted to find a new recipe for bread pudding. If you enter "bread pudding recipe" into your favorite search engine, you will probably get around 1,700,000 results in less than a second. With such a general search, you will see many of the same sites listed because those sites have several recipes for bread pudding. If you traditionally use AllRecipes.com, you will get 5,000 recipes for bread pudding. You may not care to look at more than 5,000 recipes, but the point is that the variety of data (in this case, recipes) available is far greater than 5,000 because information is being sourced from everywhere.

Here is another way to look at it. From the perspective of a company offering a product, there is also a multiverse of options for sharing information:

- The company's website
- A PDF or other downloadable/printable document containing information about the product
- Third-party websites, which could include the manufacturer of the product (in the case of a reseller like Amazon) or other resellers of that same product (competitors)
- Other media, such as social networks

Now suppose that company offered a new product:

- They distribute information about the product through email, snail mail, social media, direct contact, and direct print.
- The information gets passed to a variety of departments for input into their specific system (catalog, sales information, etc.).

- One risk: in each case, the information is handled by a person. There is the opportunity for error.
- Another risk: an error in the initial communication. Although corrected, how many of the recipients made that same correction in their information?

You can see this is a less-than-perfect system, but it's what we have. So how is information in the Internet of Things universe best handled?

The basic problem is the way information is shared. The manufacturer (or other entity) initiates information but in a generic fashion, not attuned to the school and its students. This could present problems. And other issues exist.

Internationally, different nations have different guidelines for how information is obtained and shared. Countries following the guidelines established by the European Union demand specific privacy options for their citizens—whether participating online from Brussels or as visiting faculty to your site.

Other locations may use another currency. Or they may have different laws regarding how information is presented on the web. They may have different agencies through which products must be filtered. Unless you and your sources of information have considered this, there is much room for errors.

One possible method of control is to have all information based in the company. Invitations are sent out to *retrieve* the information from the controlled company database. Specific guidelines are set up regulating the way that information is handled by the distributors and other interested parties. By providing others with a *connection* to the information, a control factor is implemented. While there are no perfect solutions, understanding the issues involved is a good first step.[4]

NOTES

1. Janssen, Dale, and Cory Janssen. N.d. "Embedded System." *Technopedia*. Accessed June 2, 2018. Retrieved from https://www.techopedia.com/definition/3636/embedded-system.
2. Astronomy Program, University of Texas at Austin. 2018. "McDonald Observatory—the University of Texas at Austin." Accessed April 27, 2018. Retrieved from http://www.as.utexas.edu/mcdonald/mcdonald.html.
3. Sharma, Rahul. 2017. "Big Data Analytics and Sensors: How They Are Transforming Our World." *TechGenix* magazine, November 16, 2017. Retrieved from http://techgenix.com/big-data-analytics/.
4. Modera. 2010. "Managing Information in the Digital Multiverse." Whitepaper delivered at the CIO Summit 2010, February 23–25, 2010, Bremen, Germany. Retrieved from https://www.modera.com/upload/_Managing_information_in_the_digital_multiverse.pdf.

Chapter Eight

The Security Nightmare

So what happens when hackers turn their attention to connected planes, trains, automobiles, and beyond? Connected devices will be and have been hacked. Statewide education and research networks are constantly targeted for digital break-ins, from novice cybersecurity pranksters to sophisticated collaborators seeking to gain scientific, medical, and military research data.

Educause is arguably the top professional association for information technology in higher education. As the curator of the all Internet addresses ending in *.edu*, Educause is well respected by university and college CIOs. Within its grouping of "2018 Top 10 IT Issues," Educause named information security as the number-one concern for college information technology (IT) departments. The finding concluded that nearly 70% of its college respondents were working to develop "a risk-based security strategy that keeps pace with security threats and challenges."[1]

Although the categories of threats on a campus may or may not change as a result of intelligent, embedded technologies, the potential impact of Internet of Things (IoT) attacks will need to be faced even as new strategies are developed. Having a teacher or student leave a door unlocked is one thing. But having a hacker with the ability to unlock all doors or any door at will is an exponentially more serious situation. Worse yet, a potential shooter with the ability to lock doors through the network must now be planned for in a college's emergency response.

According to Zach Supalla, who runs his own IoT company, Particle IO,[2] steps are being taken to mitigate risk. Each new generation of IoT devices includes stronger encryption algorithms and other forms of security. As a rule, it has been the older IoT applications and installations from several years ago that have been featured in the more negative news.

The human element will continue to be involved as a major, correctable aspect of security. According to Joseph Yazdanpanahi, simple actions such as a student losing an unprotected cell phone or an employee stepping away from his or her computer for a quick coffee break without logging out can open the door to harm.

Standards for IoT information sharing and practice, or a lack thereof, present another roadblock to progress. For example, to realize their full potential, robotic cars need to talk to each other, to traffic signals, to parking facilities, and so forth. By 2025, that could happen. However, a car's range will be limited to where common or interchangeable standards are in place. The cars will need to work through a common platform, or at least compatible platforms, in order for the devices to speak and understand a common digital language.

Opines Bill Franks, the chief analytics officer at Teradata, "While it is possible that pushing toward standards could slow some things down in the short term, I believe that it will enable a lot more value in the long term."[3]

MORE THAN JUST THE MACHINES

Much online security is based on machine-to-machine communication. This means one machine or IoT device exchanges information with another. For example, if you sit in your office and have a video call with a colleague in a distant state, your computer and your colleague's are exchanging information. Cybercriminals are diligent in their search for ways to breach these types of communication channels. When they succeed, catastrophic invasions into personal information databases occur.

Machine-to-machine security is stronger than ever, but threats still exist. Today, most security breaches are built to prey upon an uninformed online user. Someone who inadvertently clicks an unsafe link or responds to an illegitimate message opens the door and invites a hacker in. Both browsers and email programs are now more sophisticated, so it has become harder for attacks to break through. Rest assured, however, that for every safeguard, someone is out there trying to figure out how to get around it. And failing to update software or computer operating systems keeps the newest safeguards from protecting the computer. This is where the greatest vulnerability lies.

What does this mean for the Internet of Things? Beecham Research[4] has looked at the current security environment and what can be expected as the

YOUR MOST COMMON SECURITY THREAT? SOCIAL ENGINEERING

By Joseph Yazdanpanahi

Social engineering is the art of manipulating people in order to gain access to their computer system or to information that was otherwise confidential. Whether in business or in higher education, the biggest cybersecurity vulnerability is caused by untrained employees and co-workers. Just a single miscue by a careless or unsuspecting teacher or administrator can render most traditional cybersecurity efforts useless.[a]

On the popular social discussion website Reddit,[b] there is a subsite called "Act Like You Belong." This website highlights people who were able to get someplace they should not be just by looking the part and acting confident. We all remember the two people who snuck into a White House party and took a picture with President Obama without being invited.[c] With this in mind, how easy would it be to sneak into your workplace and act like you belong, potentially causing threats to your network?

During a visit to a friend at the hospital, a gentleman told the nursing staff that he needed to get on their computer. "I am with IT," he told them. They all moved out of the way and were willing to let him access their important systems; he then confessed that he was just a visitor and was just having a bit of fun. They were all shocked at how easily they were duped.

It doesn't take a genius to be a hacker. In 2008, a 20-year-old college student guessed Sarah Palin's Yahoo! email password and gained unauthorized access. He used her birthdate to answer one of the standard security questions and then looked through all her emails. One kid still in middle school was criminally charged after shoulder-surfing his teacher's administrative-level password and logging into the computer.[d]

Historically, some of the most commonly used passwords is "password" or "12345." Furthermore, every time a major website is hacked, very few people change their passwords, leaving themselves vulnerable as people commonly use the same password on multiple sites. The website haveibeenpwned.com allows you to search your personal login information against over 4.8 billion accounts from over 251 data breaches.

Malicious emails and phone scams are a daily occurrence because they are so highly effective. A caller to human resources, identifying

(continued)

herself as the school superintendents' office, was emailed hundreds of staff members' payroll information, including bank account and social security numbers. It is important to always think critically and skeptically.

Social engineering takes on many different forms beyond confidence fraud and hacking. Trusting malicious websites or attachments in emails, plugging in unknown flash drives that someone maliciously left behind, and trusting others with confidential information are all forms of a manipulative means to an end. Some people prey on common fears—for instance, by threatening that you will be arrested if you do not give your bank account details or passwords.

It is important to ensure that the employees in your organization are equipped with training to combat the growing threat of social engineering. A single point of failure can open your entire network to data theft, data loss, or destruction of costly systems. Adding the complications of the Internet of Things into the mix just multiplies the options for damaging campus systems or accessing student and employee records with dire consequence.

Joseph Yazdanpanahi is the CIO for the City of Jacksonville, Texas, who formerly worked with the United States District Court for the Eastern District of Texas and with the county government in Smith County, Texas.

NOTES

a. Ponemon, Larry. 2017. "State of Cybersecurity in Small and Medium Businesses." Keeper. Retrieved from https://keepersecurity.com/2017-State-Cybersecurity-Small-Medium-Businesses-SMB.html.

b. Reddit. 2018. r/Act Like You Belong. Accessed June 28, 2018. Retrieved from https://www.reddit.com/r/ActLikeYouBelong/.

c. Weisman, Jonathan, Suzanne Vranica, and Shira Ovide, 2009. "White House Party Crashers Cause a Hangover." *Wall Street Journal*, November 28, 2009. Accessed June 28, 2018. Retrieved from https://www.wsj.com/articles/SB125934769738866723.

d. Goodin, Dan. 2015. "BUSTED—Eighth-Grader Charged with Felony for Shoulder-Surfing Teacher's Password." Ars Technica, April 10, 2015. Accessed June 28, 2018. Retrieved from https://arstechnica.com/information-technology/2015/04/eighth-grader-charged-with-for-shoulder-surfing-teachers-password/.

world moves toward the broader IoT spectrum. Related to the current computer security environment:

- Most current threats are aimed at networks or individual machines, not at machine-to-machine communication.
- Security solutions are designed for broad protection. This means a single solution can protect networks (campus wired and wireless, statewide or nationwide networks, cellular networks, etc.), platforms (where the data is stored), sectors (consumer, retail, health care, transportation, education, etc.), system operators (those who create and maintain the programs that keep your network up and running), and end users (you).
- Most security solutions are easy for an IT department to understand, control, and maintain. Yet departments need to be staffed and/or supported to account for the threats.
- Security levels are designed to match the demand placed by the number of users, the number of devices, the typical activity for the users, and the security level needed. For example, student records may need greater security than library databases—you want adequate security but managed within the budget.

By the same account, IoT-related security focuses even more specifically:

- Looking constantly at the expanding demand. Protecting not only users, but a constantly expanding number of devices. For example, your home thermostat or wireless door lock.
- Connecting many users and sectors. Not only can a user employ many devices but he or she can access other devices and the World Wide Web from anywhere. A single user can be connected to health care, education, and transportation within a short time frame.
- Providing access to higher-value combinations of information and control. From a smart device, users perform banking transactions, view personal health records, and make stock trades.
- Promising greater value and impact to users, operators, and attackers. The more the world is connected, the more we rely on that connection. But that also means a greater opportunity for cybercriminals to look for vulnerabilities.

THREATS TO YOUR NETWORK

The malicious software known as *malware* is another hazard. What is malware, and what does it do? Malware includes spyware, computer worms, Trojan horses, and other viruses and unwanted infections.

The first known computer virus was created, in a controlled environment, in 1971. Malware was present a decade or more before home personal computers (PCs) became popular. In 1982, the Elk Cloner virus made an appearance. The popularity of the PC and the use of floppy disks to install programs and store information made the spread of the virus easy. It was a benign virus, so although computers were infected, no problems resulted. In 1986, the Brain virus began spreading. Originated as an antipiracy measure, the virus has the effect of making some disks unusable due to timeout errors.

In 1988, the Morris worm hit. It took advantage of an operating system flaw, and within a day took down the Internet as it existed then. It was also credited with ultimately bringing down 6,000 computers. In 2000, the I Love You worm ultimately created over $15 billion in damage globally.

As the 21st century dawned, more and more people were using the Internet. Online ads and online shopping increased. People were getting paid for ad clicks. Infections of spyware and adware exploded. In 2006, Zeus malware appeared. It used basic social engineering to trick people into clicking email links, unwittingly allowing the creator access to login information, PIN codes, financial details, and more.

By 2007, more malware was being created every year than had existed in the entire history of malware. Malware writers had to come up with a way to install the threat automatically. That is when exploit techniques, social engineering, and using macros in PowerPoint and Excel became much more sophisticated. By 2010, not-for-profit malware all but died out. For-profit malware became almost exclusive.[5]

SPECIFIC INFECTION TYPES

Having mentioned several infection types, here are a few additional details:

Spyware—Spyware can infect not only your desktop but your laptop, your tablet, and even your smartphone. The purpose of spyware is to spy. It gathers information about your usage habits, including logins, credentials, personal email addresses, and so forth.[6]

You can become infected in a number of ways. Some websites may attempt to load spyware when you visit, or you may get a pop-up that asks for your permission to download software. Read these notifications carefully, do not simply click through the warnings.

Infection may come as part of a software download, particularly "free" software. Read the installation notifications carefully. You will often get something you did not want, whether it is spyware or something else. Avoid impatiently clicking through all the warnings. "Free" software always carries a price.

Infection may even occur with antispyware software. This does not mean all antispyware software is bad, but if you ever get a pop-up that tells you your computer is infected, delete it. These usually occur when browsing the web.

Spyware can infect any operating system, so do not think your Mac is safe.[7] Pay for a legitimate antispyware application. Some will protect your smartphone as well.

Worm—A computer worm is self-replicating software that duplicates itself to spread to uninfected computers.[8] A worm works in the background. It does not rely on a user to do anything; it looks for security vulnerabilities and then replicates itself within a network. Its primary purpose is to overwhelm the network or even the entire Internet. Once a computer or server is infected, the worm uses that server or computer to send out inquiries to other computers or networks. An ultimate target is usually identified, such as the U.S. government or a particular financial institution or online retailer. Overwhelming the online sales of a retailer is a method of preventing online business from occurring. If the online retailer's server is overloaded with bogus requests, legitimate customers cannot get through.

Trojan Horse—A Trojan horse essentially allows an unauthorized user access to your device. If you notice unusual activity on your computer or changes to computer settings that you did not make or activity on your computer when it should be idle, you may have a Trojan horse infection.[9]

Trojan horse infections trick the computer into thinking the activity is a normal process. You can get a Trojan horse in several ways. Again, "free" games and other "free" downloads are often carriers. The truth is that not all free downloads on the Internet are bogus, but do your own research and use caution.

Trojan horse infections can also occur with messaging. You may get a message that includes a photo or other graphic. Be absolutely certain that message is legitimate before clicking the attachment.

Trojan horse infections can occur via email. Be keenly aware of language, spelling, grammar, and so forth in any message you receive, particularly if the message is uncharacteristic of the sender. An email with a simple "Thought you would enjoy this" and a link is a good example. Clicking the link may invite an infection.

As with any other threats, a solid, legitimate security application is well worth the money.

Ransomware—Once a computer is infected with ransomware, the user cannot access files, or may not be able to get past the warning screen, until the ransom is paid. The ransom message often instructs the user to pay a fine by credit card or using online currency (such as bitcoin). Amounts could be small or reach into thousands of dollars.[10]

Ransomware is often spread through phishing email messages. Phishing is an online ploy that makes the user think it is a legitimate request. For example: "Your bank account has been frozen due to suspected activity. Click the link below to enter your credentials and unfreeze your account." One, a bank would never notify you via email and would never ask you for credentials online. Clicking the link may appear to do nothing, but the ransomware (or other infection) now has the access it needs.

Ransomware infection can also occur through a visit to an infected website. Attempting to find free music or free movies is a good way to open the gateway to all manner of malicious software.

There are an estimated 1.8 billion websites as of January 2018.[11] Unfortunately, this includes many that are created for the purpose of spreading malware. Use common sense in your web browsing and protect your devices with a reliable security application.

PREVENTION

How do you prevent infection? College campuses spend thousands of dollars a year for multiple layers of protection. Do the physical gatekeepers and software-based virus protections and spam blockers catch everything? No, but configured correctly, they do catch a majority of malware infections. Being aware and being cautious yourself will prevent you from becoming that one computer on campus that infects everyone else.

A few very simple steps will help you protect yourself against malware.

1. Keep your computer operating system and all computer programs up to date. How many times have you ignored that *Updates Available* notification. Updates close vulnerabilities discovered by others. If you ignore updates, you're posting a welcome sign.
2. Use the firewall in your operating system. A firewall lets you control who and what comes into your computer. If you do not have it turned on, turn it on. You can control how aggressively it protects your computer.
3. Install antimalware (antivirus) and antispyware software. Many programs cover both, and many are free. But before installing a free program, read the customer reviews. Free software, including bogus antispyware products, can be the route malware travels to enter your computer.
4. Update your web browser. Many browsers now update themselves, but if you use a browser that did not come with your computer or laptop, make sure it is updated periodically.

5. Do not click links in email messages. If you are absolutely, positively certain the message came from someone you know and trust, it may be okay. But beware of messages from friends and colleagues that have short, simple messages like "Thought you'd like this"—a sure sign the message is unauthorized and dangerous. When a potential virus-laden message appears, delete it, then notify the person who sent it.

PLANNING FOR FAILURES, RECOVERIES, AND SECURITY

So what happens when everything you have put into place fails to halt the attacks and a hacker gets into your system and starts wreaking havoc? Planning for failures by developing incident responses, procedures for communicating with your students and faculty when failures happen (particularly if communication is down), and conducting simulation exercises to respond to potential threats is a good place to start.

Campuses have become astute at rehearsing their responses to storms, floods, and other natural disasters. Since Columbine, schools have likewise revamped their response plans and conducted full-scale rehearsals to prepare for the potential of a campus shooter or a less severe act of violence at their facility.

As a result of hurricanes and floods on the Gulf Coast from Florida to Mexico in the past two decades, schools have used IoT tools to keep their virtual doors open. After Hurricane Katrina, Tulane University and other schools moved courses and student participation to the web, ensuring that many classes carried on. Likewise, during Hurricane Rita and the Houston flood of 2018, Lamar Technical College and other Houston-area schools set the standards for online courses as an emergency backup plan. To the chagrin of public school students, the lessons learned have evolved today to cover snow days and other school closings.[12]

Planning for technology failures, particularly as IoT becomes more common, will develop with a similar urgency. What happens when an IoT welding tool is externally reprogrammed to operate at unsafe temperatures; when lights are shut down during a night class; or when all points-of-sale scanners on campus malfunction or record the wrong information? What happens when an extreme burst of Internet traffic from campus cell phones crowds out the bandwidth needed for onsite registration or a final exam? How will your IT and even your frontline faculty and staff respond?

Students and staff can and should be involved in developing the responses. With new apps, security-conscious students are already being integrated into the response systems for campuses. Cell phone apps are rapidly being deployed to allow students or others on campus to directly broadcast from their phones into the school security system. Call-911 integrated apps such as Red Guardian and Blackboard Connect are examples of tools that are gaining some prominence.

During a campus emergency, an act of violence, or a student injury, the apps quickly expand the capabilities of the professional responders. As adoption rates for various apps tends to spike following an emergency, public consciousness of major hacking events or prominent security breaches will continue to motivate cybersecurity planning and response exercises.

THE PROFESSIONAL EDGE

As the focus of this book is the impact of Internet of Things and not a direct treatise on security, you can easily research the large amount of material and other books out there on the campus network security. Like the response to physical threats on campus, you can never be prepared enough or spend enough time and money to prevent every incident.

Vendors and consultants can help, but be aware that there is a built-in incentive for them to create and maintain a level of fear to direct your investments. Use common sense. Every dollar applied to security may be pulling funds away from the academic enterprise and the true mission of your college. At the same time, you do know the costs that can be created should systems be down during peak registration or finals.

Maintaining professional links and ensuring that your technical staff are involved with other educational and technical professionals who can offer unbiased advice is a vital part of a good security plan. Although $1,500 or $2,000 duplicated several times annually may seem to provide a significant hit to a campus budget, it can easily pay for itself when your staff is able to prevent an attack or better judge the tools needed within the network. Associations like Internet2 (www.internet2.edu), Educause (www.educause.edu), the ITC (www.itcnetwork.org), and state or regional research and education networks (www.internet2.edu/communities-groups/members/research-education-networks/)[13] offer an unbiased option and multiple sources of information through session and personal networking that, again, make a membership fee an inexpensive investment.

Working with staff prior to their participation with an organization or within a training event can simultaneously increase the value of your college's investment. Work with your staff in advance to set goals that they can achieve during and following their participation. Upon their return, provide a forum where they can share the new information and offer potential action steps considered during the experience. Incorporating follow-up into their personal assessments can also convert the new knowledge into action.

Monetizing a staff member's participation illuminates the impact. Although some employees are better at assessing value than others, encourage employees to work with their supervisors to estimate value based on their participation in training or professional association activities. If a training event was useful in identifying a new tool that can cut costs, note that and identify the value. If a threat that would impact the campus is identified and can be prevented as a result of training, estimate what the cost of an incident could have been and report the potential savings in the follow-up report.

The bottom line is that security is manageable and will continue to be as the Internet of Things develops. New threats and abuses will occur, but each event will also come with a new set of lessons and create new tools for moving forward.

Even better, the security threats promise to create a lot of career options for the graduates of the next decade. From firewall engineers to ethical hackers, careers are coming into play that were unheard of even five years ago.

NOTES

1. Grajek Susan, et al. 2018. "Top IT Issues Infographic." Educause. Accessed June 24, 2018. Retrieved from https://www.educause.edu/research-and-publications/research/top-10-it-issues-technologies-and-trends/2018.
2. Buntz, Brian. 2016. "When Will the IoT Security Discussion Grow Up?" Internet of Things Institute. Accessed June 24, 2018. Retrieved from http://www.ioti.com/security/when-will-iot-security-discussion-grow.
3. Whyte, Alisa Valudes. 2015. "The Future of the Internet of Things Is Amazing, If We Don't Muck It Up." *Huffington Post*, November 25, 2015. Updated November 25, 2016. Accessed June 24, 2018. Retrieved from https://www.huffingtonpost.com/alisa-valudes-whyte-/the-internet-of-things-future_b_8640360.html.
4. Beecham Research. 2017. "IOT Security Threat Map." Accessed June 25, 2018. Retrieved from http://www.beechamresearch.com/download.aspx?id=43.
5. Martindale, Jon. "From Pranks to Nuclear Sabotage, This Is the History of Malware." Digital Trends, March 29, 2018. Retrieved from https://www.digitaltrends.com/computing/history-of-malware/.
6. Malwarebytes. N.d. "All About Spyware." Accessed April 1, 2018. Retrieved from https://www.malwarebytes.com/spyware/.
7. Evans, Jonny. 2018. "Warning as Mac Malware Exploits Climb 270%." *ComputerWorld*, March 12, 2018. Retrieved from https://www.computerworld.com/article/3262225/apple-mac/warning-as-mac-malware-exploits-climb-270.html.

8. Rouse, Margaret. 2017. "What Is a Computer Worm?" Search Security, TechTarget Network, June 2017. Retrieved from http://searchsecurity.techtarget.com/definition/worm.

9. Rouse, Margaret. 2018. "What Is Trojan horse?" Search Security, TechTarget Network, January 2018. Retrieved from http://searchsecurity.techtarget.com/definition/Trojan-horse.

10. TechTerms. 2017. "Ransomware Definition." April 21, 2017. Retrieved from https://techterms.com/definition/ransomware.

11. Tek Eye. 2018. "How Many Websites Are There in the World?" Accessed June 25, 2018. Retrieved from http://tekeye.uk/computing/how-many-websites-are-there.

12. Ford, Nicole. 2018. "No More Snow Days: School Districts Replacing Snow Days with Virtual Classes." ABC8 News, August 1, 2018. Retrieved from https://www.wric.com/news/national/no-more-snow-days-school-district-replacing-snow-days-with-virtual-classes/1339240298.

13. DiMaria, Frank. 2016. "Tapping into Research and Education Networks." CampusTechnology, August 11, 2016. Retrieved from https://campustechnology.com/articles/2016/08/11/tapping-into-research-and-education-networks.aspx.

Chapter Nine

The Careers of the IoT Age

Johnny had been at his terminal for several hours when a message started flashing in front of him. As his workstation regularly monitored his breathing, heart rate, body temperature, and facial indications of fatigue, it was time to take a break. A stretch would ensure he stayed healthy and keep his total effectiveness up. Still, Johnny was really into the details of what he was doing and also had a habit of getting fixated within the data stream.

A hand on his shoulder and a not-unexpected voice broke in. "Ready to go for a walk, Johnny?" The break intervals attuned to Johnny's vital signs and biorhythms were mandatory. The system automatically halted any new calls, and the work in progress not deemed critical was delayed.

"C'mon. The gang's all out in the courtyard waiting for you. They've got a bean bag toss going on just calling your name." Aiden was the health coach for Johnny's workgroup. As a wellness advisor for the team, it was his role to monitor their moods and levels of motion to attain peak performance and job satisfaction. Aiden himself was actually an employee of the company's insurance provider.

"Of course. You know I like being out in the courtyard. Especially on a nice day like this."

They wandered from the terminal to the break room. The outside doors opened as they approached and strolled into the lush courtyard. Others were milling about, playing bocce, ping-pong, and Johnny's favorite, the bean bag toss. Any type of game was allowed, as long as it did not require looking at a screen or hologram.

Once Johnny returned to his station, his and Fred's conversation and education started anew. "You know, every long-haul truck used to have at least one person onboard and driving it. They even had sleepers attached to the cab so one person could rest while another drove."

Johnny looked at Fred like he was crazy. "Really? Why did they do that?"

"People used to drive cars, too. Everybody had one. At one time it was a status symbol. I guess some people never got over that."

Johnny shook his head. "I can't imagine. If I need a ride somewhere, I just tap my wrist band and a car comes to get me."

Fred smiled. "We could kind of do that. They called those taxis—but they had drivers in each of them. A lot of times, you took your chances with the folks who did the steering. Guess you never heard the term 'like a bat out of hell.' Some of them would drive like mad."

Johnny pondered this historical information. "I guess a lot of people had jobs that don't exist anymore, right?"

"They did. Warehouses had workers who would load things onto trucks. Trucks had to be maintained and repaired. Before machines were built that diagnosed problems and rebuilt engines or other components and when cars required fluids that were replaced by hand, people had jobs that did all of that. Other truck drivers delivered the items to the customer. All those jobs are now obsolete."

There were even entire industries dedicated to creating and moving replacement parts around. Before 3-D printing started, there were companies for auto parts, machine parts, computer parts, plumbing, and electrical devices. You name it and there was a business built around it. It seems like it was almost overnight that suddenly any smaller item that was made out of wood, plastic, or metal could be created on the spot—and all of those businesses were gone.

"What happened to those people?" Johnny never knew harsh poverty. Such a thing really was not a part of his world.

"New jobs came along. People to program the trucks. People to build, maintain, and repair the robots. People to build, maintain, and repair the drones. The whole world has changed in the last twenty years. But it seems that as long as you don't mind learning a little or going back to school, you can find a job. Just like the one you're doing now."

Johnny remembered something one of his friends said. "Fred, you ever heard of a doorbell?"

"DADDY, WHAT'S A TRUCK DRIVER?"

Much has been made of the predicted decline in the common jobs of today, such as truck drivers, cabbies, and delivery personnel. As robotic vehicles progress, many of today's transportation-related roles will diminish or disappear. Other changes brought on by the Internet of Things (IoT), including 3-D printing and a redistribution of warehousing infrastructure around the country, will further change the nature of long-haul and local delivery.

An evolving of the new age will be far from limited to the blue-collar arena. The U.S. Department of Labor's Occupational Projections for 2026[1] show significant growth in several energy-related areas, in medicine and health care, and in business. Yet specifics in those fields will vary, quite often due to Internet-driven technologies. Chief executive officers are projected to see a 4% decline in their numbers as technology pushes corporate consolidation to fewer locations and automation handles more of the decision making that no longer goes to the top offices. Executive assistants, likewise, will continue to contract, again as a result of embedded Internet technologies automating their functions.

Assembly-type positions, in engine and machine repairs, aircraft construction, textile work, electronics assembly, and metal and plastics work will continue to decline, as jobs are enabled or replaced by Internet-driven robotics. There may still be a future "in plastics" but most likely as a raw material for 3-D printing rather than with labor-intensive factory production.

HEALTH CARE

Across the board, health care appears to be a safe bet as a career choice for the next decade. Even for executive assistants and secretarial work, medicine is one of the few major fields where employment will continue to grow. An aging population, a demand for longevity and extended care by patients, and trends toward universal coverage will continue to place demands for a larger medical workforce through the 2020s.

Personal care aides, registered nurses, home health aides, medical assistants, and licensed vocational nurses will continue to be among the fields showing the largest job growth at least through the middle of the decade. And by percentage, physician assistants and nurse practitioners will show a greater than 30% rate of growth and with an average salary exceeding $100,000. Physical therapists and their related assistants will increase in number by more than 25%, with nursing and health specialty teachers at close to the same rate.[2]

Relying on health care as a sure thing comes with caveats. Medical devices, phone-based medical apps, and the emerging of "tele-doc" technologies will eat away at medical employment from the opposite end. The Bureau of Statistics reports show a decline in fields such as respiratory therapy technicians, the second-fastest declining occupation in the nation, decreasing by 56% over the 10-year period leading to 2026.[3] The declining rate is in opposition to the growing rate of respiratory therapists (23%), indicating that the assistants are being replaced by the newer technologies and an ability by the therapists to build those into their professional practice.

Over the longer term, the replacement of the "technician" roles in medicine will likely expand into the more professional areas. In 2018, the Mayo Clinic partnered with Corindus Vascular Robotics, Inc., to pilot "telestenting," a remote, robotic-driven stenting procedure to repair blood vessel and artery failures.[4] Could such studies portend the movement of many or even all surgeries to nonhuman practitioners in the future? If so, what does that mean for the medical profession and for upcoming jobs in the medical fields?

Diagnosis, once an exclusive domain of the physician, seems almost destined to move down the chain of command. A reason for the growth of nurse practitioners (nurses with advanced training allowing them to practice medicine and prescribe medications) along with physician assistants (who can do the same under the supervision of a licensed MD) is their expansion into the realm formerly held by the family doctor.

IoT technologies, likewise, will continue to alter the roles played by physicians as cell phones and related apps replace the general practitioner for initial diagnoses. Phone-based medical apps continue to roll through both the U.S. Patent Office and the Food and Drug Administration. The result is a phone that is quickly turning into Dr. McCoy's Star Trek Tricorder, the sci-fi handheld device that could diagnose most medical conditions.

Phone apps are available or in the works to take blood sugar and diabetes readings, conduct full-body ultrasounds, monitor for arrhythmias, and visually examine a stray freckle for melanoma. As an app is approved and put into practice, diagnoses are one step closer to occurring at the point of the patient. Costs per examination are reduced significantly, although most patients will use the services with far greater frequency. Real issues will reach the physician earlier, and treatments can start right away.[5]

A literal million-dollar question is will the result be more or fewer office visits? And what will be the impact on the jobs involved in diagnosis and treatment? The answers are coming. As a certainty, the working roles will change even more and in an unpredicted fashion over the next decade and a half.

SO WHAT IS NEXT?

The role of the futurist is less to predict the future than it is to generate options. By generating ideas and following options to a logical conclusion, futurists can identify pathways and construct strategies for when the options play out.

At the turn of the century, few would have predicted a major terrorist attack on New York City within two years. Some had, however, and, for better or worse, stood ready with plans as the events unfolded. From an educators' perspective, the second wave of activity from the event had more of a direct impact on students' lives. The careers generated in response added new and unexpected options in airport and border policing, military contracting, and Middle Eastern languages.

Likewise, science and engineering discoveries since 2005 led to an increased use of hydraulic fracturing or "fracking." The result was a revival of the oil exploration and extraction industry in the United States. Shaking off a mantle of energy dependency, the country became a net exporter of petroleum products. Oilfield jobs boomed, housing prices in oil towns increased, and the national market dynamics around imports and exports changed drastically. Again, the occurrence was not widely predicted.

On the other hand, within today's IoT field, futurists and predictions of what lies ahead abound. Although any prognostication should be taken with a grain of salt, projections of eight or more years ahead can only look at possibilities.

For the eighth grader of today, career options and opportunities approaching 2030 will be different. Careers will be shaped by the predicted advances in technology and altered by the unexpected event. Looking ahead, here are some of the more optimistic and the less Pollyannaish possibilities.

At the 2017 World Economic Forum, Microsoft pioneer Bill Gates offered his predictions in technology, economics, and world health.[6]

In health care, while Mr. Gates saw the conquering of plagues such as polio foreshadowing the defeat of other diseases, he cited epidemiologists who believe that man-made threats through bioterrorism could dwarf the death toll of 9/11. At the same time, a new "green revolution" through technology and science with a focus on Africa could end hunger, with the continent becoming agriculturally self-sufficient.

The digital revolution with IoT, artificial intelligence, and communications technology will continue to reshape the Third World. Between universal mobile banking, worldwide access to clean and cheap energy, and shared learning, most of the developing world's population will escape the worst forms of poverty.

In response, the working world will change. Automation, predicts Gates, could replace millions of jobs. The creation of new, more rewarding jobs, along with the way work is managed and taxed, will have to follow suit.

ARTIFICIAL INTELLIGENCE

Artificial intelligence (AI), argues Google CEO Sundar Pichai, is becoming so profound in its impact that it could be compared to fire or electricity. Seeing the potential for AI to cure diseases or solve the energy crisis, Pichai noted that jobs like attorneys or accountants may soon no longer be needed. Jobs using AI technology, however, should be poised to grow.[7]

How is artificial intelligence related to the Internet of Things? Consider how your IoT-enabled home thermostat works. The "learning thermostat" monitors when you leave and when you return, then programs itself to raise or lower temperatures accordingly. Externally accessing information online, like the current outside temperature or humidity, it can adjust the conditions in your home. As it monitors how you change the settings at different times of the day or following different activities, it learns your preferences and can adjust accordingly in the future.

Its connection to the Internet allows you to modify settings or check its status from your handheld device anywhere on the planet.

Your phone's GPS app is another example. A global positioning system app connects with multiple satellite and other markers to "learn" your most common routes, projecting distance and the length of time for a commute. Integrating information it gathers from online traffic and weather reports while identifying potential stopping points based on your past stops and driving habits, GPS is one of the most remarkable and useful combinations of AI and IoT.

Starting with GPS, self-driving vehicles are all about artificial intelligence, relying on your input to provide a destination, watching online and through its built-in sensory tools for traffic patterns and road construction, and, most important, for communication with a centralized core of driving information.[8]

Since Stanley Kubrick's *2001 Space Odyssey* and Nena's American version of "99 Red Balloons," the concept of artificial intelligence connected to weaponry has been generating bad dreams. On the plus side, a rifle that recognizes fingerprints could prevent harm to children from a parent's improperly stored weapon. Drones with an ability to set their own targets, however, could fail and cause harm in a number of outcomes. Automated responses to an escalating battle, as in the "99 Luftballons" lyrics, could lead to the doomsday scenario.

Perhaps just as frightening in its own way, intelligent marketing algorithms have been built into a number of your devices. Whenever you go to a company website, your phone or browser is marked with an electronic cookie—alerting the marketing team to your interest and directing you to related products. If you are tied into a Google Home or an Amazon Echo device, it is generating data on you with each exchange and adding to its intelligence related to your interest and behavior.

A glance at the projected value of the artificial intelligence market in a few years offers a strong insight into future job trends. PricewaterhouseCoopers (PwC) estimates the global economic impact of AI over the next decade could exceed $15 trillion.[9] Artificial intelligence will replace a lot of jobs, but how many jobs are being created with a specific focus on AI-related development, manufacturing, and production? And will AI allow society to change enough to open more careers for the creative and fine arts?

How many trainers and educators will be employed to help users understand and create with their new devices? Education as skills training, life coaching, and human resource development will be a huge part of this growing segment. Anything that is created in the IoT and AI environment will be expected to come with a number of "how to" options. Videos to demonstrate how it works, online trainers to help with the details, and helpdesk staff—both AI and live—who can work you through any remaining issues.

There is still a lot of work to do to have a fully functional, rational robot that can think like a human, but progress is happening. Machines with human-level intelligence are anticipated in about three or four decades, but that is with a lot of givens—one of the greatest that emotional intelligence can be reproduced similarly to logic and calculations.

Work that requires empathy will be slower to move to devices and artificial responders. Creative endeavors, things that require multiple levels of consideration and response, are also going to be around for a while.

So how long is "a while"?

QUANTUM COMPUTING

Thinking of artificial intelligence, quantum computing is a natural tie in. Quantum physics, quantum mechanics, and quantum computing are built around the physical attributes of light. Albert Einstein and others helped to prove that light could act as either a particle or as a wave. Going beyond the traditional work in computers where processing and memory happen as a binary option—bits are either turned on or off—a quantum scenario allows the wave function within a bit to offer more options. *Wired* magazine says this could result in processors that could "operate 100,000 times faster than they do today."[10]

The technology leap provided by quantum computing and other advances in computer memory and processing technologies is a key to taking artificial intelligence and embedded technologies to the next levels. Career paths and academic programs exploring machine intelligence, quantum computing, and electrical engineering as a result will offer some great outcomes.

As quantum computing and artificial intelligence will drive the future of technology, producing a reliable connection through the Internet will do the same. Technology fields supporting interdevice communication with advances in device security developed to protect that communication have a huge potential.

WORK AND THE SELF-DRIVING CAR

In early 2018, two fatal car accidents involving self-driving cars stunned the nation. In Arizona, a pedestrian was struck and killed. In California, a vehicle driver was killed. In both cases, the "autopilot" was engaged and yet the car did not stop.

How will similar fatalities impact the move to self-driving cars? On the plus side, the United States currently logs approximately 40,000 traffic fatalities per year. How many of those lost lives would have been saved by a car smart enough to avoid a collision?

Wikipedia's "History of Autonomous Cars"[11] notes that self-driving cars have been in the works for nearly 100 years with very few accidents. The irony is that the number of successful test runs and implementations of self-driving vehicles does not make the news, only the failures do.

In 2009, Ford introduced the self-parking feature as standard on some models. Google has been working on self-driving cars since 2010, and by 2013 their cars had traveled over 500,000 miles. Two years later, Tesla brought forward its Model S, basically self-driving but requiring a driver to monitor the car's reactions and to override the automation when trouble occurs.[12]

In a 2018 fatal crash, records showed the driver failed to heed visual and audible warnings inside the car and did not keep his hands on the wheel. This brings to mind the joke about the driver who put his recreational vehicle on cruise control, then strolled back to the kitchen to make a sandwich. The biggest problem with these earlier driverless cars was the driver assuming the car was far more capable than it was. Just because a car has adaptive cruise control, blind-spot monitoring, lane-departure alert, and lane-departure steering correction does not mean it will actually drive itself.

Still, a broader approach for self-driving age for cars is emerging. It will impact more than just the automobiles themselves.

Self-driving cars will have a tremendous impact on the insurance industry. The Internet of Things has already had an effect on insurers, with the introduction of insurance phone apps, immediate and understandable comparisons of rates and features, and the implementation of intelligent voicebots to take customer claims in lieu of live attendants.

The net result of self-driving cars, however, will be a much lower number of drivers behind the wheel, reduced vehicle ownership, and a major decline in highway accidents and deaths. Car insurance rates will decline substantially,

Figure 9.1. Partnering with Tesla and other manufacturers, California's Rio Hondo College rebuilt its Automotive Technology program to support alternative fuels, autonomous vehicles, and other IoT innovations. New careers will continue to emerge as others disappear due to the Internet of Things. ***Photo courtesy of John Frala from the Rio Hondo website at http://www.riohondo.edu/altfuels/***

accidents will become far less common, and repairs due to accidents will be far fewer in number. Personal car sales will give way to fleet sales, more leased autos (or a leased service using the nearest car to pick you up and deliver you) and shared car ownership.

Understanding upcoming careers will require keeping an eye on where technology is going. How are educational institutions preparing graduates for careers in artificial intelligence, quantum computing, or autonomous vehicles? Where the varied fields have been separated in the past, they all now have the commonality of a dependency upon the new technologies.

IBM's CEO, Ginni Rometty, said: "Every job will require some technology, and therefore we will need to revamp education. The K–12 curriculum is obvious, but it is the adult retraining—lifelong learning systems—that will be even more important."[13]

Fred Lokken, the chair of the American Association of Community Colleges' Instructional Technology Council and the compiler of the annual *Trends in eLearning* community college survey, tells his millennial students to plan to change careers at least eight times in their lifetimes. Constant retraining and adult education, says Lokken, have already become the norm.[14]

Learning to manage the coming levels of transition should be a priority for students. Planning for job endings and how to create a new career should even become a part of the standard college curriculum, say authors Heather McGowan and Chris Shipley. By learning to "embrace uncertainty, students and workers of the IoT Age can better ride the employment market."[15] Referring to IoT as the fourth industrial revolution, McGowan and Shipley urge educators to teach agility, preparing their students for a 90-year active life span.[16]

Somewhat by 2030 and even more so by 2040, the concept of completely retiring at 60 or 65 will be a remnant of a 60-year lifespan and a blue-collar past. Careers will become more fluid, with individuals moving in and out of regular employment throughout their lifetimes. Concepts such as a minimum universal basic income are already in place in areas of Europe and will be brought into play in parts of the United States as automation and embedded technology further drive the economy.[17] As the remainder of the developed world has embraced universal health care, the United States will also generate its own unique form to support the workforce in a fluid labor market.

EMERGING CAREERS

Looking 80 or 100 years into the past, it is hard to imagine grandparents and great-grandparents considering the worker of today gainfully and respectfully employed. In the early 1900s, the large majority of the workforce was employed in farming or agricultural support, lacked any use of electricity, and had not yet enjoyed television or radio. Days were spent working behind a horse-drawn plow, bending over to pick crops, or toiling over a wood-fired stove to cook the day's meal and to prepare canned or dried foods for storage. Factory workers, more often than not, lived out their own versions of a Charles Dickens novel.

The hardworking, information-centric employee of today would not have seemed to be working at all to a laborer prior to the First World War. Sitting at a desk, watching moving pictures on a screen, reading? Most likely, it would have seemed quite frivolous to a West Virginia coal miner. Add the concepts of personal vehicles, air-conditioning, indoor plumbing, and microwave ovens, and the perception would be that no one had a real job.

You may have a similar perception of the career path of a Gen Z or a millennial student moving forward. Even today, most people have job titles or are performing tasks that were hardly imagined in the 1980s. By 2030, most of today's students will be pursuing fields that have yet to come into existence. And by today's standards, it is likely that you might not consider the new fields work at all.

So what are some of the latest jobs? The U.S. National Science and Technology Council recently published a projection of priorities for advanced manufacturing to provide guidance to upcoming federal allocations and funding proposals. Five emerging areas of manufacturing technologies were identified as priorities:

- Advanced Materials Manufacturing
- Engineering Biology to Advance Biomanufacturing
- Biomanufacturing for Regenerative Medicine
- Advanced Bioproducts Manufacturing
- Continuous Manufacturing of Pharmaceuticals[18]

You may note four of the five areas are directly connected to aspects of medicine and health care, although advanced bioproducts manufacturing could also impact agriculture, computer technology (biologically driven computer memory), and construction/engineering.

Looking toward the areas needing intensive efforts to promote innovation, eight areas were identified:

- Additive Manufacturing
- Advanced Composites
- Digital Manufacturing and Design
- Flexible Hybrid Electronics

- Integrated Photonics
- Lightweight Metals
- Smart Manufacturing
- Revolutionary Fibers and Textiles
- Wide Bandgap Electronics[19]

Six of the areas for innovation directly encompass the Internet of Things, while the remaining three, dealing with composites, metals, and textiles, involve materials that will be involved in embedded-technology constructions.

THE DISCONNECT WITH TEACHING

Many argue that there is a clear disconnect between what students gain from higher education and the needs of the workplace. Few employers care whether graduates earned a 4.0 grade point average. They want to know if the graduate has the ability to fill an open position and to continue growing and adapting with the business. The market wants people who have the skills, can work collaboratively, get along with others on the team, and have the drive needed to generate ideas and to be successful. In many educational institutions, that "drive to succeed" is focused on grades, working in teams is rare, and collaboration is viewed by many instructors as cheating.

The commentary "Learning Innovation in the Digital Age" from the *McKinsey Quarterly*[20] highlights both the challenges and opportunities facing educators today. Topics included:

Partnerships—Colleges have difficulty keeping up with the latest technologies and innovative approaches on their own. Jointly managed partnerships with specific industries could help colleges stay on the cutting edge.

Focus on Skills—The heavy focus on degrees and completion at many schools has been achieved at the expense of providing marketable skills. Funding based on degree completion rates are dead ends for innovators, who tend to tackle a course or program for specific skills, then drop (at least for a time) when the immediate need is met. Then, although a transcript may offer a list of courses, that may or may not offer any depth of information on the competencies or qualities gained within a given class.

Lifelong Learning—Continuing instruction and learning beyond the initial degree is a key to individuals who want to remain relevant and in leadership roles. Colleges and universities that wish to remain relevant likewise have to determine how to incorporate lifelong learning into the core of their operations.

A CAREER IN CYBERSECURITY: IS IT RIGHT FOR YOU?

By Deppy Thompson

Cybersecurity refers to a unique set of strategies and techniques used to protect computer systems, networks, and programs from unauthorized access, damage, and attack. According to Forbes, *the global cybersecurity market is expected to reach 170 billion by 2020*.

In today's connected world, a cyberattack can result in an individual experiencing identity theft, extortion, or loss of important data. On a broader level, critical infrastructure like power plants, hospitals, and financial service companies can be affected. On a global level, cyber threats can affect the military, political or infrastructural assets (through cyberterrorism, cyberwarfare, and cyberespionage). Securing all data, whether on a personal or a national level, is crucial to keeping our society functioning smoothly.

Keeping up with cybersecurity strategies and techniques can be a challenge, as attackers are now launching sophisticated attacks at lower and lower costs. The last few years have shown a dramatic uptick in sophisticated threats and malware. Companies and organizations worldwide are now facing the challenge of finding skilled cybersecurity professionals who can outpace advanced threats, as there are more devices than people and attackers are becoming more creative than ever.

Adam Vincent, CTO–public sector at Layer 7 Technologies (a security services provider to federal agencies, including Defense Department organizations), describes the problem: "The threat is advancing quicker than we can keep up with it. The threat changes faster than our idea of the risk. It's no longer possible to write a large white paper about the risk to a particular system. You would be rewriting the white paper constantly."

"For many years, the focus has been on perimeter defense and defending the walls of the castle," says Eddie Schwartz, the international vice president of ISACA, chair of ISACA's Cybersecurity Task Force, and president and COO of WhiteOps. "The emergence of security professionals that can cope with advanced threats and advanced adversaries hasn't kept up with the changes in cybersecurity. Right now, many organizations try to solve this problem on their own, and they try to hire people," he says. "It is sort of like a bunch of small countries trying to fight a superpower in terms of organized criminals and nation-states; there's just no hope."

Skills shortages in cybersecurity are widespread. The "State of Cybersecurity: Implications for 2015" study reports that fewer than 25% of cybersecurity applicants are qualified to perform the skills needed for the

(continued)

job due to a lack of credentials and the ability to understand the business. The main reason is that the skills required to fight cyber threats are very different from those that are needed for conventional IT security.

Some technology proponents are looking to higher levels of automation (and point toward moving away from manual processes). "Automation is a good thing if you can get there from here," says Schwartz. "Our industry, security, has not perfected predictive analytics yet; we are not even close to getting there, and artificial intelligence isn't here yet either. So, I think for a long time to come, we are going to see the need for humans to be deeply involved in the cyber security process, particularly when it comes to stopping events."

Training and certifications that equip candidates to actually perform the skills needed are gaining momentum. According to a report by job analytics firm Burning Glass Technologies, job postings in cybersecurity have grown three times faster than those for IT jobs overall, and cybersecurity professionals are earning 9% more than their IT counterparts.

If cybersecurity interests you, start by exploring the various careers that are offered in this field:

- **Ethical Hacker.** Ethical hacking (also known as penetration testing) is a proactive form of information security. Businesses and organizations hire ethical hackers to help improve their networks, applications, and other computer systems in order to prevent data theft and fraud. One of the first examples of ethical hacking occurred in the 1970s when the U.S. government used "red teams" to hack its own computer systems.
- **Cryptographer.** Cryptography keeps messages and other data secret and away from the prying eyes of criminals or enemy governments by using mathematically based encryption methods. A cryptographer is someone who develops algorithms, ciphers, and security systems to encrypt sensitive information and provide privacy for people and corporations.
- **Security Architect.** A security architect is a senior-level employee who is responsible for designing, building, and maintaining the security structures for an organization's computer system. Thinking like a malicious hacker helps a security architect become adept at understanding and anticipating the moves and tactics that a hacker might use.
- **Security Engineer.** As the company's first line of defense against unauthorized access from outside sources and potential security threats, security engineers have a very important job to do. Not only do they know how to pinpoint any potential threats, they also know how to plan and prepare before any security threats take place.

- **Computer Crime Investigator.** A computer crime investigator can look at various crimes, ranging from hacked or damaged file systems on computers to crimes against kids. Computer crime investigators are also able to recover and gather electronic evidence and data from computers that can be used in prosecuting crimes.
- **Chief Information Security Officer (CISO).** Also known as a global head of information security, a CISO is a senior-level executive within a company who is responsible for setting out and executing a security program in order to make sure a company's information and technologies are protected from both internal and external threats.

And the list continues. Other working titles include

- IT Security Consultant
- Information Security Analyst
- Information Security Auditor
- Information Security Director
- Security Software Developer
- Security Systems Administrator

Many experts suggest that someone interested in cybersecurity begin with a job, internship, or apprenticeship in IT. This will provide the fundamentals such as administering and configuring systems, networks, database management, and coding. It also offers an understanding of IT procedures and real-world business operations.

IT jobs that can lead to cybersecurity careers include

- Computer Programmer
- Software Engineer
- Technical Support Specialist
- Computer Systems Analyst
- Database Administrator
- Network Administrator
- Computer Network Architect
- Computer Systems Administrator
- Web Developer

Journalists, please write press@sokanu.com for more information.

Deppy Thompson is the cofounder of Sokanu, a career test and platform designed to measure people's intrinsics and match them to careers. She is also a regular blogger at https://www.sokanu.com/blog/.

This article was revised from a blog post that originally appeared on March 7, 2018, at https://www.sokanu.com/blog/career-in-cyber-security/.

NOTES

1. U.S. Bureau of Labor Statistics. 2018. "Employment Projections: Occupational Projections and Worker Characteristics." *Occupational Projections Data 2016–26*. Accessed June 9, 2018.

2. U.S. Bureau of Labor Statistics 2018.

3. U.S. Bureau of Labor Statistics 2018.

4. Corindus Vascular Robotics, Inc. 2018. "Corindus to Participate with Mayo Clinic in Preclinical Study of Remote Control Robotics for Percutaneous Coronary Interventions Remote Treatment Capabilities." Press release, January 4, 2018. Retrieved from http://www.corindus.com/news-events/press-releases/corindus-to-participate-with-mayo-clinic-in-preclinical-study-of-remote-control-robotics-for-percutaneous-coronary-interventions-remote-treatment-capabilities.

5. Murgia, Madhumita. 2017. "How Smartphones Are Transforming Healthcare." *Financial Times*, January 12, 2017. Retrieved from https://www.ft.com/content/1efb95ba-d852-11e6-944b-e7eb37a6aa8e.

6. Waller, Chris. 2017. "Bill Gates Is Pretty Good at Predicting the Future. This Is What He Thinks Will Happen Next." *Business Insider*, May 8, 2017. Retrieved from https://www.weforum.org/agenda/2017/05/bill-gates-is-pretty-good-at-predicting-the-future-this-is-what-he-thinks-will-happen-next1.

7. Goode, Lauren. 2018. "Google CEO Sundar Pichai Compares Impact of AI to Electricity and Fire." *Verge*, January 19, 2018. Retrieved from https://www.theverge.com/2018/1/19/16911354/google-ceo-sundar-pichai-ai-artificial-intelligence-fire-electricity-jobs-cancer.

8. Neiger, Chris. 2018. "9 Facts about Artificial Intelligence That May Surprise You." *Motley Fool*, January 31, 2018. Retrieved from https://www.fool.com/investing/2018/01/31/9-facts-about-artificial-intelligence-that-might-s.aspx.

9. Reo, Armand S., and Gerard Verweij. 2017. "Sizing the Prize: What's the Real Value of AI for Your Business and How Can You Capitalize" [download]. *PWC*. Retrieved from https://www.pwc.com/gx/en/issues/data-and-analytics/publications/artificial-intelligence-study.html.

10. Beall, Abigail. 2017. "Laser Breakthrough Could Make Computers 100,000 Times Faster." *Wired UK*, March 13, 2017. Retrieved from http://www.wired.co.uk/article/ultrashort-light-pulses-quantum-computing.

11. Wikipedia. 2018. "History of Autonomous Cars." Accessed July 25, 2018. Retrieved from https://en.wikipedia.org/wiki/History_of_autonomous_cars.

12. Lewis, Dan. 2017. "The History of Driverless Cars." The Fact Site, June 2017. Retrieved from https://www.thefactsite.com/2017/06/driverless-cars-history.html.

13. Friedman, Thomas L. 2018. "While You Were Sleeping." *New York Times*, January 16, 2018. Retrieved from https://www.nytimes.com/2018/01/16/opinion/while-you-were-sleeping.html.

14. Lokken, Fred. 2018. "The Futurology of Distance Learning: Are You Prepared for What Is Coming Next?" NETnet Summer Distance Learning Conference, June 15, 2018, Mt. Pleasant, TX.

15. McGowan, Heather, and Chris Shipley. 2017. "The Future of Work: Learning to Manage Uncertainty." OEB Insights, August 25, 2017. Retrieved from https://www.linkedin.com/pulse/learning-uncertainty-imperative-heather-mcgowan/.

16. McGowan, Heather, and Chris Shipley. 2017. "Preparing Students to Lose their Jobs." LinkedIn, October 25, 2017. Accessed June 17, 2018. Retrieved from https://www.linkedin.com/pulse/preparing-students-lose-jobs-heather-mcgowan/?trackingId=QpmHDPwcbr0b%2BsgYFrHa%2FQ%3D%3D.

17. Kingma, Luke. 2018. "Universal Basic Income, the Answer to Automation?" Futurism. Accessed June 17, 2018. Retrieved from https://futurism.com/images/universal-basic-income-answer-automation/.

18. Subcommittee for Advanced Manufacturing. 2016. "Advanced Manufacturing: A Snapshot of Priority Technology Areas across the Federal Government," pp. 4–39. National Science and Technology Council, April 2016. Retrieved from https://www.whitehouse.gov/sites/whitehouse.gov/files/images/Blog/NSTC%20SAM%20technology%20areas%20snapshot.pdf.

19. Subcommittee for Advanced Manufacturing 2016, 4–39.

20. McKinsey & Company. 2017. "Learning Innovation in the Digital Age." *McKinsey Quarterly*, September 2017. Retrieved from https://www.mckinsey.com/business-functions/organization/our-insights/learning-innovation-in-the-digital-age.

Chapter Ten

Looking Ahead

If all you have is a hammer, then every problem looks like a nail.

The authors, in looking at the issues and opportunities facing higher education over the next 30 years, have chosen to look at the coming changes through a lens of embedded technologies and the Internet of Things (IoT). Just as easily, they could have, and to some degree have indeed, looked at the emerging student experience through artificial intelligence, pathways to employment, or emerging curricula. Each of the perspectives would be legitimate.

The exploration of technology's impact on higher education, our classes and our students, is much like John Godfrey Saxe's poem "The Blind Man and the Elephant." Godfrey, a relic of the old British Empire, described six "men of Indostan," all examining an elephant without vision. As the men approach the animal from different angles, each has a unique perspective:

> The sixth no sooner had begun, about the beast to grope,
> than, seizing on the swinging tail, that fell within his scope,
> "I see," quothe he, "the elephant is very like a rope!"
>
> And so these men of Indostan, disputed loud and long,
> each in his own opinion, exceeding stiff and strong,
> Though each was partly in the right, and all were in the wrong![1]

By focusing on the future of higher education from a perspective of the Internet of Things, you should have begun to see opportunities where they may not have existed while spotting threats that otherwise would have been missed. Your approach to education should change. New embedded tools and apps will be integrated into your classrooms and your curriculum.

Teaching methods will change, too, as IoT tools are used by your students with a professor's blessing and guidance, no longer viewed as crutch or a distraction.

Whether initiating new construction or renovating older facilities, it is now in your capacity to consider how IoT technologies impact both the process and the outcome. Can new building automations create savings or improve services sufficiently to justify the added cost? Will changes in student behaviors, personal vehicle ownership, and the need to be physically on the campus change the demands and nature of your physical plant?

A report from the Global Agenda Council on the Future of Software and Society, through the World Economic Forum, predicted a number of technology trends by 2025.[2] The following are trends related to education:

1. **How People Connect**—The technologies and methods people use to connect with those around them, to information and to the Internet of Things, is transformative. From smartwatches to Internet-enabled lenses, personal technologies will create an almost magical capacity for the individual through technology.
2. **Omnipresent Computing, Communication, and Storage**—Changes in cost, capacity, and connection to data storage and interconnection will create an explosion in the growth and potential of the Internet. Cloud services will become "ubiquitous" as everyone is able to tie into a supercomputing capacity from their personal devices.
3. **The Internet of Things**—IoT will likewise become pervasive, as embedded sensors become "smaller, cheaper and smarter." Integrated into your clothes, and throughout your daily world, the technology will affect the workplace, the home, and the social environment. Career options will change, likewise restructuring the nature of leisure and recreation.
4. **3-D Printing**—The initial impact for colleges as 3-D printing gains wider deployment and becomes cheaper is that schools will stockpile a smaller inventory of parts and supplies, decreasing storage needs and waste. Like with IoT, however, 3-D printing will impact the careers students prepare for. Retail space with face-to-face sales will continue to decline, and manufacturing of smaller products will diminish. Careers will shift to the creators of new designs and to those who can figure out how to make the systems work, from governmental regulators who determine where a product is taxed from when constructed in the home, or if tariffs are involved when a product design comes from abroad yet is produced on a local printer.
5. **Analytics and Artificial Intelligence (AI)**—The massive collection of data about every event and every participant will offer an ability to predict

actions, direct behavior, and react to events in a fashion never before experienced. Software that can mine the data while learning from it is new. As AI is increasingly embedded into IoT devices, the management of automated events will increasingly move from centralized servers into the embedded devices themselves.

NETWORKING FUTURES

As to the future of the campus network, there are mixed perspectives on where IoT and other technologies are leading. Although recent trends have seen data centers and other network management structures centralizing in the cloud, there are those who describe it as a different type of centralization. Where once a campus might have a single networking center, virtual servers and high-speed wide-area networks have allowed campuses to consolidate management sites, coordinate storage with state networks or with software vendors, and even to offload their data remotely to a commercial data storage center used by tens and hundreds of varying clients.

External connectivity will remain and become even more vital. As a connection is needed for every aspect of campus life, from the student information system to managing inventory in the cafeteria to security monitoring on the college grounds, it will become increasing impossible to work without a connection and a live Internet service. Multiple Internet providers will become a must, as an outage can mean closing many of the services of the school.

Other backups are on the horizon. Machine intelligence and embedded technologies continue to become more powerful, allowing localized processing to occur at routers, gateways, and in IoT devices independently of a centralized controller. Using SWARM technologies within an IoT context, activity may still happen nearer to the user. The smart switches, routers, bridges, and gateways, however, can connect many devices, making all of their resources available to a collective intelligence.[3] The broader deployment of telehealth services and robotic cars over the next decade will also lead for a push for more networking options and infrastructure to serve even the most rural areas.

RESOURCES FOR THE EDUCATOR

By this point, you have let your interest be stirred enough to stay abreast of the Internet of Things. There are a number of professional associations, organizations, and publications that can also help you keep up with what is next. Some of the best groups mentioned from earlier chapters include

- **The Instructional Technology Council (ITC)**—An affiliated council of the American Association of Community Colleges (AACC), ITC is the only council of AACC directly dealing with the issues of technology and learning leadership. With a primary focus on eLearning and distance education, the council also sponsors a New Initiatives Group, a brain trust of innovators from colleges throughout the United States and Canada. Coordinated by one of the authors, the New Initiatives Group provided background and a sounding board for many of the issues in this writing (www.itcnetwork.org).
- **Educause**—Highlighted earlier in the security discussion, Educause targets higher education information technology (IT) leadership and staff yet has professional activities and publications for the general college administrative team. Educause has produced several specific documents on IoT with titles such as "7 Things You Should Know about the Internet of Things"[4] or "The Internet of Things, IoT Systems, and Higher Education."[5]

  Educause is also the publisher of the *NMC Horizon Report*,[6] an excellent annual document detailing the technology and technology trends foreseen to impact higher education within a five-year timeline (www.educause.edu).
- **The United States Distance Learning Association (USDLA)**—With a number of sectors under its umbrella, USDLA offers professional development and human networking support for higher education, public and private K–12 schools, military, health-care providers, and industry. Another strong feature of the organization is its use of state and regional chapters. Most likely, there is one near you (www.usdla.org).
- **The Gartner Group**—Best known for its tool, the Gartner Hype Cycle, charting the ascendance and decline of technical innovations, the Gartner Group is a publicly held company that provides IT assessments for businesses and corporations throughout the world. Of great benefit are their trend insight reports, covering multiple topics, including IoT[7] (www.gartner.com).
- **Virtually Inspired**—With a mission to offer a worldwide perspective on online courses and technology-enhanced programs, Virtually Inspired has created an online catalogue of best practices "indicative of the 'Online Classroom of the Future.'"[8] A product of Drexel University Online president Susan Aldridge and USDLA president emerita Marci Powell, Virtually Inspired displays IoT and other applications, from mind labs

to immersive games and from drone training to underwater classrooms (www.virtuallyinspired.org).

- **Internet2**—The Internet2 community initially was created as a research and education network (REN) to support research institutions with advanced networking and scientific research. Today, its mission has expanded to include a K–20 initiative, telehealth connections, and collaborative university/industry partnerships. Often partnering with state, regional, and university system RENs, significant growth has occurred since 2010, and the network now provides multiple 100 Gbps connections, interconnecting states from coast to coast (https://Internet2.edu).
- **The League for Innovation**—Also with a focus on two-year colleges, the League for Innovation offers a partnership for professional development and multicollege projects. Targeting lay faculty and administrators as much as the IT and technical support teams, the league offers a location where you can learn about innovation but with far less technical jargon. Although their largest event is the annual Innovations Conference, the annual Learning Summit offers colleges an opportunity to work as a team to construct campus solutions.

FINAL WORDS

As noted in the introduction, the greatest challenge in writing on a contemporary topic such as the Internet of Things is staying current with the material long enough to go to publication. It was interesting to view all of the changes that occurred during the book's construction.

No sooner had the authors drafted a comment such as "No, IoT is not yet at the stage of the Jetson's flying cars," than Uber announces plans to debut a deployment of a flying taxi service at the beginning of the next decade, with full deployment by 2025.

When the graphic of the "Internet of Things on the College Campus" was first developed for Chapter 7, the collective impact of the drawing surprised most administrators who saw it. Over just a few months, more and more recognize that the components are already in place on their campuses or are under consideration. The speculative nature of the truck convoy in Chapter 6 will likely pass through a number of changes and variations prior to actual deployment. Will company-based drones be able to maintain the speed to stay with a robotic trucking convoy? Will legislation follow robotics to allow speeds of 90 mph? And when will residential flying car services be viable enough to replace the personal car?

Still, the speculation and examples are provided so that you can analyze and consider your college's potential. The exacts of the convoy's technologies may vary, but the need for redundant connectivity and the changes ahead for the transport and vehicle industries are certain. And they are paralleled by the needs of education.

When the first draft of Chapter 3, including the summation of a Truthfinder .com report, was shared with its first readers, the initial response was one of shock followed with a bit of panic. Then came the Facebook fiasco with Cambridge Analytics and the releasing of subscriber personal data to political operators. The breach exceeded what was revealed in the subscription-based Truthfinder report. Nonetheless, the report has been retained, as its organizational structure offers a meaningful insight into how personal data is collected on the web and organized for use.

Shortly following the Facebook disclosure, the new European standards for personal Internet privacy took effect. California, likewise, is looking at similar state legislation. As the privacy concerns advance and legislation is interpreted and applied, the environment for IoT will change. It is hoped, however, that this book will provide the reader with insights for recognizing and adapting to the changes. And in the best of the scenarios, benefiting tremendously from the potential that lies ahead.

ONE FINAL TOOL

Be sure to check out *The Internet of Things for Educators* at www.college-iot .com for regular updates on the Internet of Things and its continuing impact on higher education, our classrooms, and our students.

NOTES

1. Saxe, John Godfrey. 1872. "The Blind Man and the Elephant." Poem Hunter. Retrieved from https://www.poemhunter.com/poem/the-blind-man-and-the-elephant/.

2. Global Agenda Council on the Future of Software and Society. 2015. "Deep Shift: Technology Tipping Points and Societal Impact." World Economic Forum, September 2015. Retrieved from http://www3.weforum.org/docs/WEF_GAC15_Technological_Tipping_Points_report_2015.pdf.

3. Taberner, Tim. 2018. "Swarm Intelligence for IoT: Greater Than the Sum of Its Parts." *Industrial Ethernet Book* 87 (12). Retrieved from http://www.iebmedia.com/index.php?id=10853&parentid=74&themeid=255&hft=87&showdetail=true&bb=1.

4. Holeton, Richard. 2014. "7 Things You Should Know about the Internet of Things." Educause. Retrieved from https://library.educause.edu/resources/2014/10/7-things-you-should-know-about-the-internet-of-things.

5. Benson, Chuck. 2016. "The Internet of Things, IoT Systems, and Higher Education." *Educause Review*, June 26, 2016. Retrieved from https://er.educause.edu/articles/2016/6/the-internet-of-things-iot-systems-and-higher-education.

6. NMC Horizon Project. 2018. *NMC Horizon Report Preview 2018: Higher Education Edition*. Educause. Accessed June 30, 2018. Retrieved from https://library.educause.edu/~/media/files/library/2018/4/previewhr2018.pdf.

7. Hung, Mark. 2018. *IoT Implementation and Management—from the Edge to the Cloud: A Gartner Trend Insight Report*. Gartner. Retrieved from https://www.gartner.com/doc/3873158?plc=ddr.

8. Drexel University. 2018. "About Virtually Inspired & Our Team." Virtually Inspired. Accessed July 1, 2018. Retrieved from http://www.virtuallyinspired.org/about-2/.

Epilogue

Graduation Day

Finally, the day arrived when Johnny officially completed his education. The college seal would appear on his bioprofile as of today, signaling his accomplishment. He planned a face call with his friends and family to celebrate. He logged in for the call, and sure enough the college seal appeared as a small symbol in the bottom-right corner of his screen. Anyone he communicated with could see it also.

Clicking on the symbol produced his accomplishment profile, including a listing of the topics he mastered. His profile showed mastery of communication, which included spoken and written language; reasoning, which included basic math and science; collaboration, which included group activity participation, working in teams, dependability, and cooperation; and leadership, which included critical thinking and embracing diversity.

His grandmother joined in. "Congratulations, Johnny. I remember when I graduated we had a big ceremony. Everyone wore a robe and we all marched into the auditorium. Then the college administrators called us up one-by-one and presented us with the diploma. We all had to make good grades because employers would look at our college transcript to determine if we were good enough."

"Thanks, Grandma," Johnny said. "What are grades, and what is a transcript?"

Fred joined the call and chuckled. "That's old stuff, Johnny. Education has changed a lot. And congratulations. Any plans for what you want to do?"

"I'm not sure, Fred. As of today, my profile includes my university skill set, and employers looking for my skills are automatically notified. I should see opportunities coming through any time."

Johnny's parents logged on. "That's great, son," Johnny's dad said. "When I graduated, I had to look for my own job. I spent a lot of hours looking online, filling out applications, and going for interviews."

Johnny's friends Cora and Susan logged on. "Wow. That sounds like a lot of work," Cora says. "So you might not find a job?"

"There were no guarantees," Johnny's grandmother said. "It was a different world."

"I'm sure you'll get something from Marble," Fred said. "You proved yourself during your internship."

Aiden, Johnny's health coach at Marble, chimed in. "Since you have a profile with Marble, your information will connect automatically and put you at the top of the list. Companies look for the best candidates, but it's always nice when that candidate is already affiliated."

"Do you have an idea of what you'd like to do, Johnny?" His mother joined the conversation.

"Fermtocomputing using quarks and gluons is making a big splash," Johnny said. "It's quite different than the old quantum computing method we use now. Becoming an expert would certainly keep me busy for at least a decade and until something else comes along."

Appendix

Truthfinder Report

How much is available about you by way of public information on the Internet. With a simple search and $29.00, one of the authors found out quite a bit about himself. This 10-page report is compressed from about 20 pages. Some names and locators have been modified for privacy protection. For $29.00, however, you can break through the privacy concerns to find this on your own...

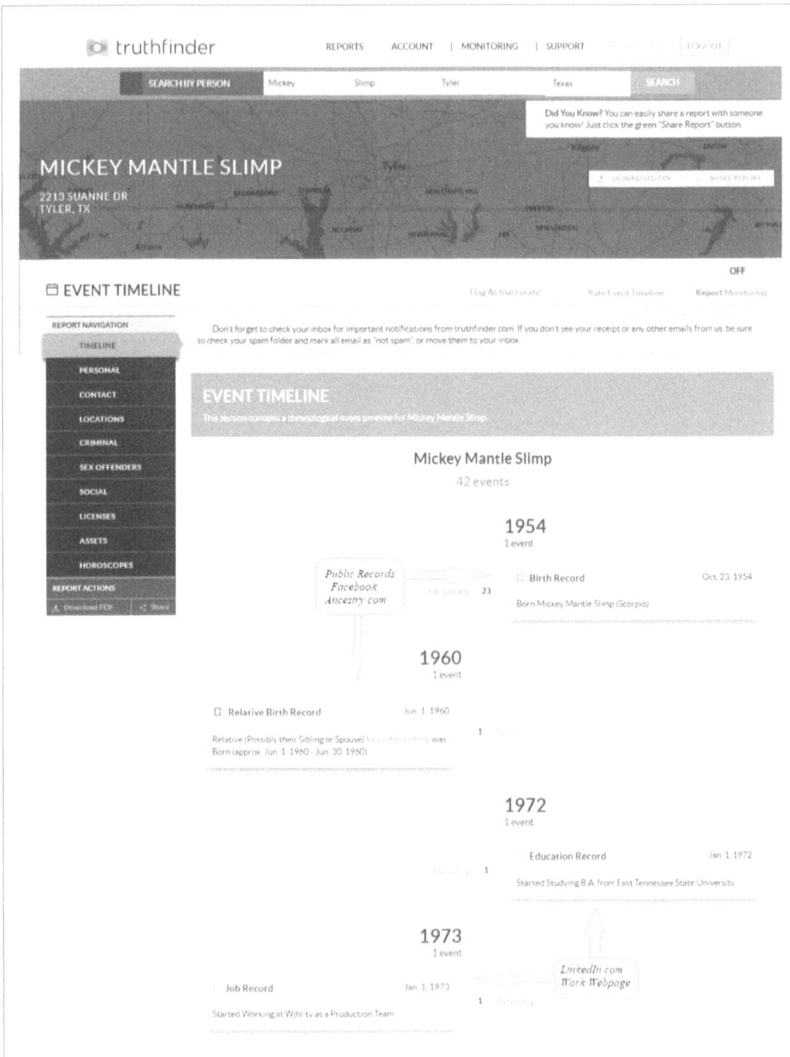

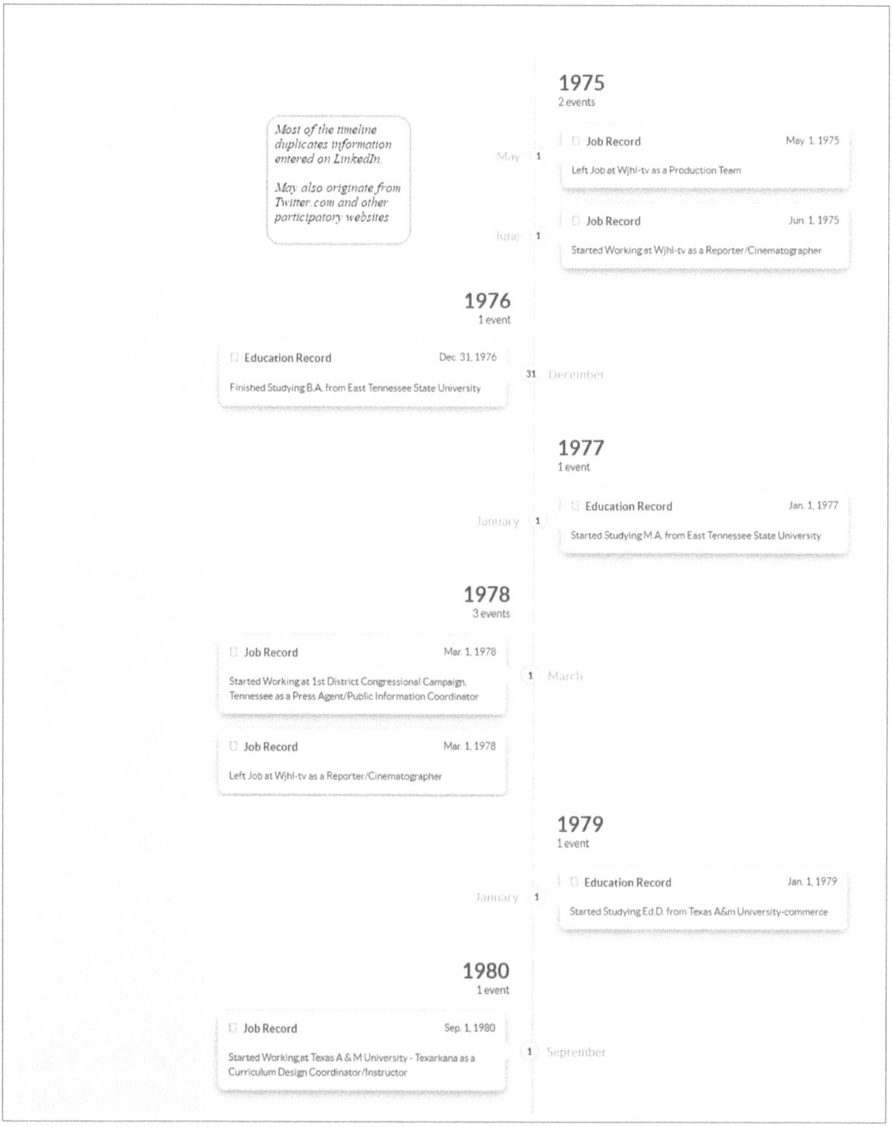

As most of the information is acquired through algorithms that pull the information directly from sites and uses artificial intelligence to make judgements on accuracy, the report will reflect issues common with the source sites. For example, LinkedIn may have difficulty distinguishing between a full-time position and an office in a professional organization, listing both on a similar level.

Past the common information sources noted here, people add to their digital footprint with every shopper's reward program or sharing a phone number with a cashier. In trade for vendor rewards and a special status, elite flyers and platinum card holders both leave a digital footprint in their wake.

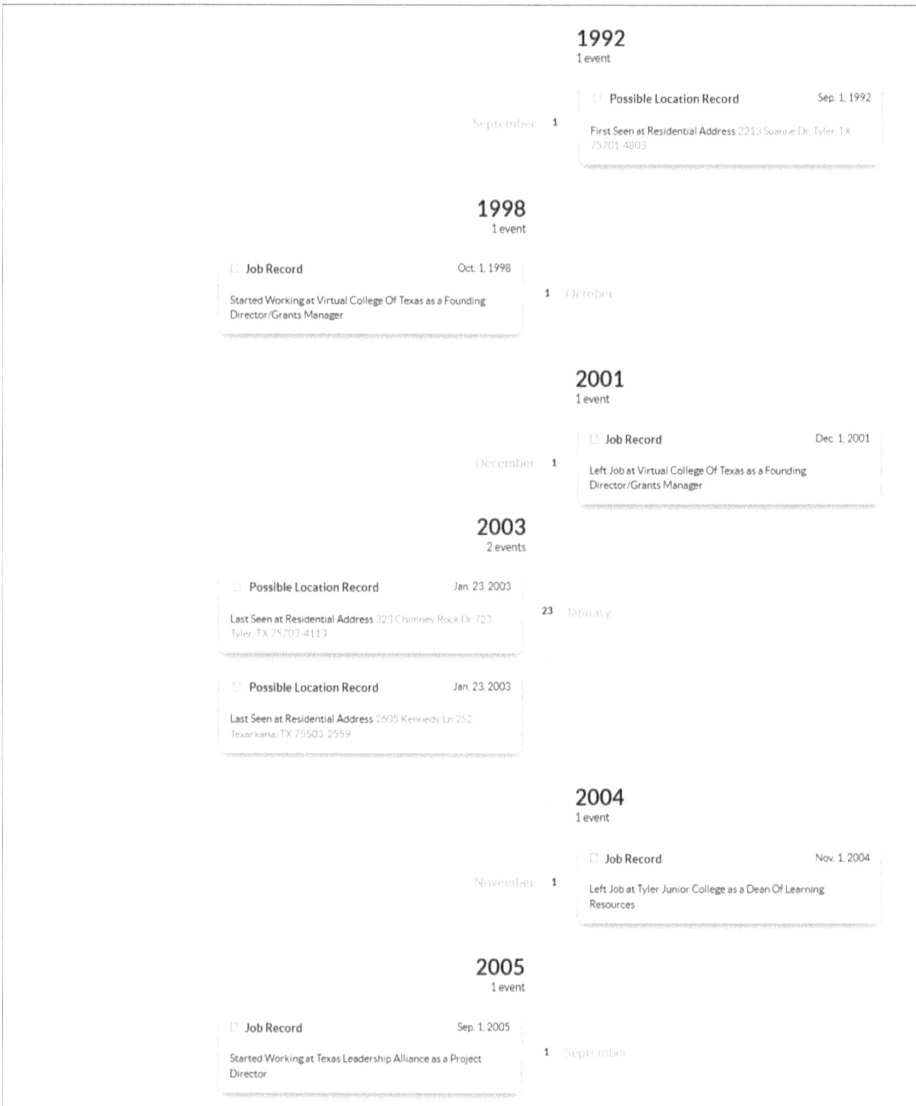

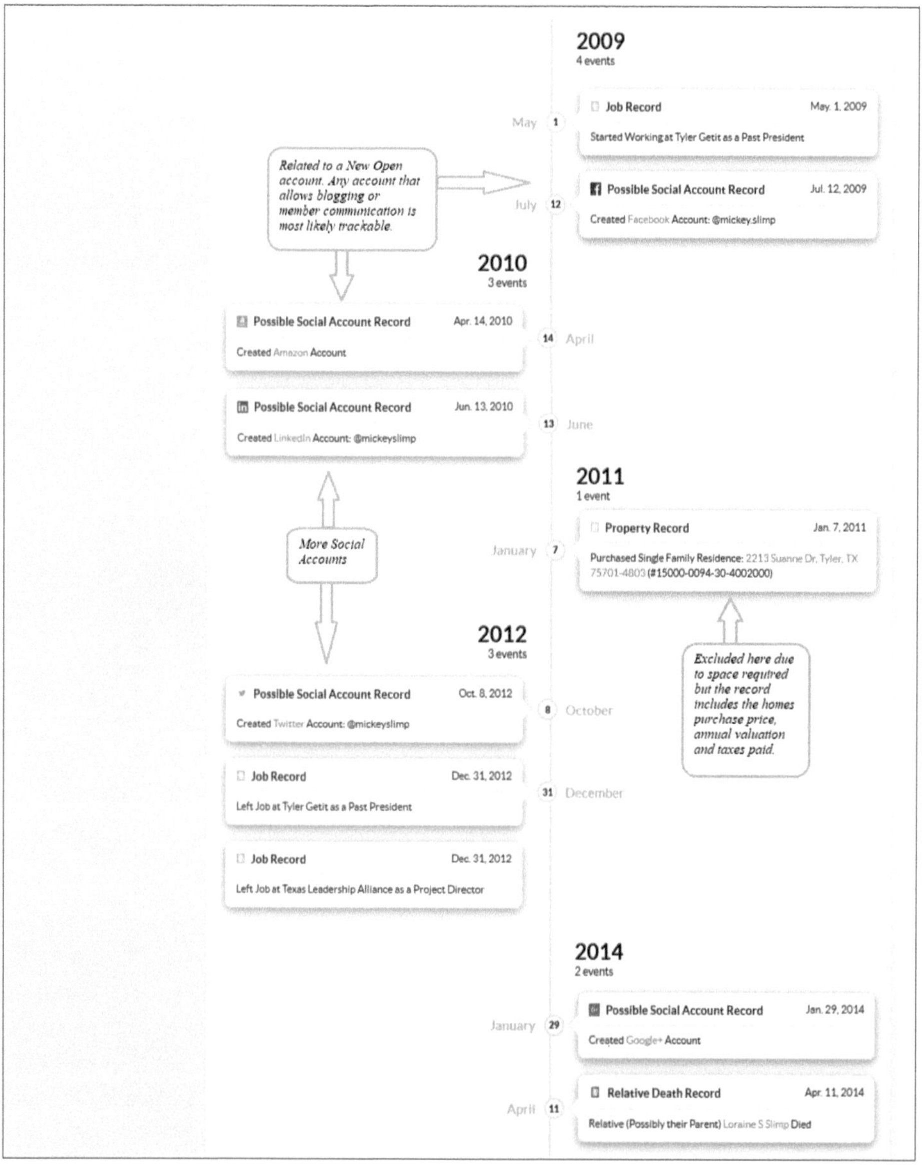
2009
4 events
May 1
Job Record May. 1, 2009
Started Working at Tyler Getit as a Past President
July 12
Possible Social Account Record Jul. 12, 2009
Created Facebook Account: @mickey.slimp
Related to a New Open account. Any account that allows blogging or member communication is most likely trackable.
2010
3 events
Possible Social Account Record Apr. 14, 2010
Created Amazon Account
14 April
Possible Social Account Record Jun. 13, 2010
Created LinkedIn Account: @mickeyslimp
13 June
More Social Accounts
2011
1 event
January 7
Property Record Jan. 7, 2011
Purchased Single Family Residence: 2213 Suanne Dr, Tyler, TX 75701-4803 (#15000-0094-30-4002000)
Excluded here due to space required but the record includes the homes purchase price, annual valuation and taxes paid.
2012
3 events
Possible Social Account Record Oct. 8, 2012
Created Twitter Account: @mickeyslimp
8 October
Job Record Dec. 31, 2012
Left Job at Tyler Getit as a Past President
31 December
Job Record Dec. 31, 2012
Left Job at Texas Leadership Alliance as a Project Director
2014
2 events
January 29
Possible Social Account Record Jan. 29, 2014
Created Google+ Account
April 11
Relative Death Record Apr. 11, 2014
Relative (Possibly their Parent) Loraine S Slimp Died

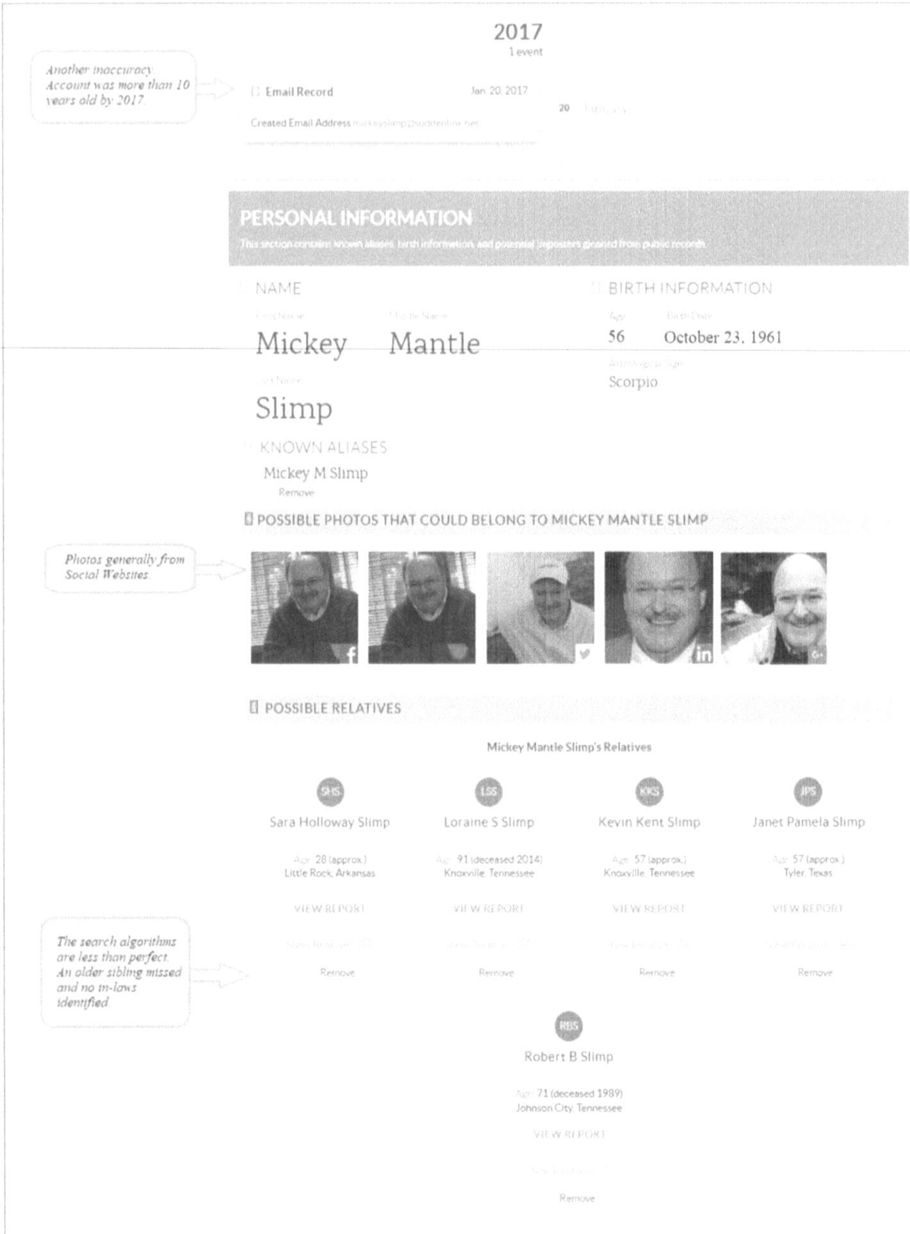

Another inaccuracy. Account was more than 10 years old by 2017.

2017

1 event

Email Record — Jan 20, 2017

Created Email Address

PERSONAL INFORMATION

This section contains known aliases, birth information, and potential imposters gleaned from public records.

NAME

Mickey Mantle

Slimp

BIRTH INFORMATION

56 — October 23, 1961

Scorpio

KNOWN ALIASES

Mickey M Slimp

Remove

POSSIBLE PHOTOS THAT COULD BELONG TO MICKEY MANTLE SLIMP

Photos generally from Social Websites.

POSSIBLE RELATIVES

Mickey Mantle Slimp's Relatives

SHS	LSS	KKS	JPS
Sara Holloway Slimp	Loraine S Slimp	Kevin Kent Slimp	Janet Pamela Slimp
Age: 28 (approx.)	Age: 91 (deceased 2014)	Age: 57 (approx.)	Age: 57 (approx.)
Little Rock, Arkansas	Knoxville, Tennessee	Knoxville, Tennessee	Tyler, Texas
VIEW REPORT	VIEW REPORT	VIEW REPORT	VIEW REPORT
Remove	Remove	Remove	Remove

The search algorithms are less than perfect. An older sibling missed and no in-laws identified.

RBS

Robert B Slimp

Age: 71 (deceased 1989)

Johnson City, Tennessee

VIEW REPORT

Remove

With the amount of information available on public sites, the standard methods of creating resumes and recruiting from blind ads is becoming an anachronism. Background checks are also available on multiple sites, including Truthfinder. Criminal records, traffic violations, and arrest records may show up in a report.

Again, the program has a limited human touch, so the report and background checks come with a number of caveats.

On a related note, the report accesses other public sites to identify and post photographs of convicted sex offenders living within the proximity of the subject.

Tax and voter rolls supply an additional list of the subject's neighbors at both current and former addresses, including their ages, approximate birthdates, and telephone.

JOBS

Company (Industry)	Job Title	Dates	
WJHL-TV	Production Team	Jan. 1, 1973 - May. 1, 1975	Remove
WJHL-TV	Reporter/cinematographer	Jun. 1, 1975 - Mar. 1, 1978	Remove
1st District Congressional Campaign, Tennessee	Press Agent/public Information Coordinator	Mar. 1, 1978 - Dec. 1, 1978	Remove
Texas A & M University - Texarkana	Curriculum Design Coordinator/instructor	Sep. 1, 1980 - Dec. 1, 1985	Remove
Tyler Junior College	Dean OF Learning Resources	Apr. 1, 1988 - Nov. 1, 2004	Remove
Virtual College Of Texas	Founding Director/grants Manager	Oct. 1, 1998 - Dec. 1, 2001	Remove
Texas Leadership Alliance	Project Director	Sep. 1, 2005 - Dec. 31, 2012	Remove
Tyler GetIT	Past President	May. 1, 2009 - Dec. 31, 2012	Remove
Northeast Texas Consortium Of Colleges & Universities (NETnet)	Executive Director	Dec. 1, 2004	Remove
UNIVERSITY OF TX HLTH SCI CTR (Hospitals)	East TX Consortium	Dec. 1, 2004	Remove
Instructional Technology Council Of The American Association Of Community Colleges	Board OF Directors		Remove
U.S. Unified Community Anchor Network (US UCAN)	Advisory Council		Remove
Lonestar Education And Research Network (LEARN)	Board OF Directors		Remove
NORTHEAST TEXAS NETWORKS CONS (College & University Placement Service)	Manager		Remove
The University Of Texas Health Science Center At Tyler	Associate Director OF Academic Administration For Student Support	Sep. 1, 2012	Remove

Variant CAPITALIZATION indicates a source other than LinkedIn for this information.

Category of employment also indicates an alternative source. Inaccuracy of data indicates it was entered by a third party

EDUCATION

ED.D. FROM TEXAS A&M UNIVERSITY-COMMERCE

January 1, 1979 - December 31, 1986

Ed.D

C&I (Educational Media & Technology

Texas A&m University-commerce

Remove

M.A. FROM EAST TENNESSEE STATE UNIVERSITY

January 1, 1977 - December 31, 1983

M.A.

Instructional Communications

East Tennessee State University

Remove

B.A. FROM EAST TENNESSEE STATE UNIVERSITY

January 1, 1972 - December 31, 1976

B.A.

Humanities

East Tennessee State University

Remove

Associates with common work or home address can be pulled again from Tax Records, workplace websites, and social networks.

POSSIBLE ASSOCIATES

People that Mickey Slimp may have shared a residential or business address with. (18 Listed)

POSSIBLE ASSOCIATE #1

Kent Willis

DETAILS

POSSIBLE ASSOCIATE #2

The site can reak havoc with the concept of a roommate. Apartment addresses can have a number of potential results. A home's past owner or prior residents may also be listed.

John Moore

DETAILS

POSSIBLE ASSOCIATE #3

Avonelle Shipp

DETAILS

POSSIBLE ASSOCIATE #4

Larry Mendez

DETAILS

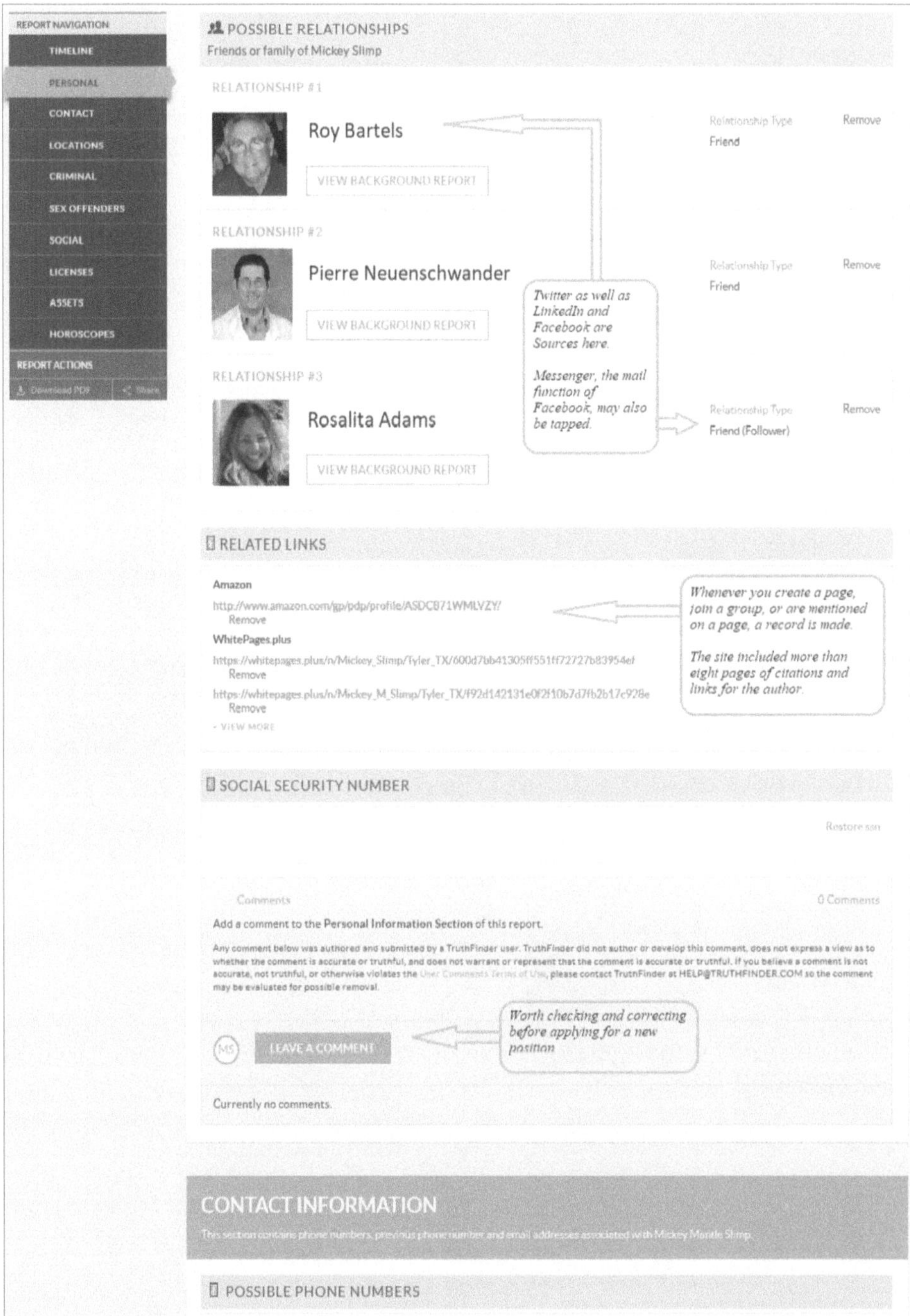
REPORT NAVIGATION
TIMELINE
PERSONAL
CONTACT
LOCATIONS
CRIMINAL
SEX OFFENDERS
SOCIAL
LICENSES
ASSETS
HOROSCOPES
REPORT ACTIONS
POSSIBLE RELATIONSHIPS
Friends or family of Mickey Slimp
RELATIONSHIP #1
Roy Bartels
VIEW BACKGROUND REPORT
Relationship Type
Friend
Remove
RELATIONSHIP #2
Pierre Neuenschwander
VIEW BACKGROUND REPORT
Relationship Type
Friend
Remove
Twitter as well as LinkedIn and Facebook are Sources here.
Messenger, the mail function of Facebook, may also be tapped.
RELATIONSHIP #3
Rosalita Adams
VIEW BACKGROUND REPORT
Relationship Type
Friend (Follower)
Remove
RELATED LINKS
Amazon
http://www.amazon.com/gp/pdp/profile/ASDCB71WMLVZY/
Remove
WhitePages.plus
https://whitepages.plus/n/Mickey_Slimp/Tyler_TX/600d7bb41305ff551ff72727b83954ef
Remove
https://whitepages.plus/n/Mickey_M_Slimp/Tyler_TX/f92d142131e0f2f10b7d7fb2b17c928e
Remove
VIEW MORE
Whenever you create a page, join a group, or are mentioned on a page, a record is made.
The site included more than eight pages of citations and links for the author.
SOCIAL SECURITY NUMBER
Comments
0 Comments
Add a comment to the Personal Information Section of this report.
Any comment below was authored and submitted by a TruthFinder user. TruthFinder did not author or develop this comment, does not express a view as to whether the comment is accurate or truthful, and does not warrant or represent that the comment is accurate or truthful. If you believe a comment is not accurate, not truthful, or otherwise violates the User Comments Terms of Use, please contact TruthFinder at HELP@TRUTHFINDER.COM so the comment may be evaluated for possible removal.
Worth checking and correcting before applying for a new position
MS
LEAVE A COMMENT
Currently no comments.
CONTACT INFORMATION
This section contains phone numbers, previous phone number and email addresses associated with Mickey Mantle Slimp.
POSSIBLE PHONE NUMBERS

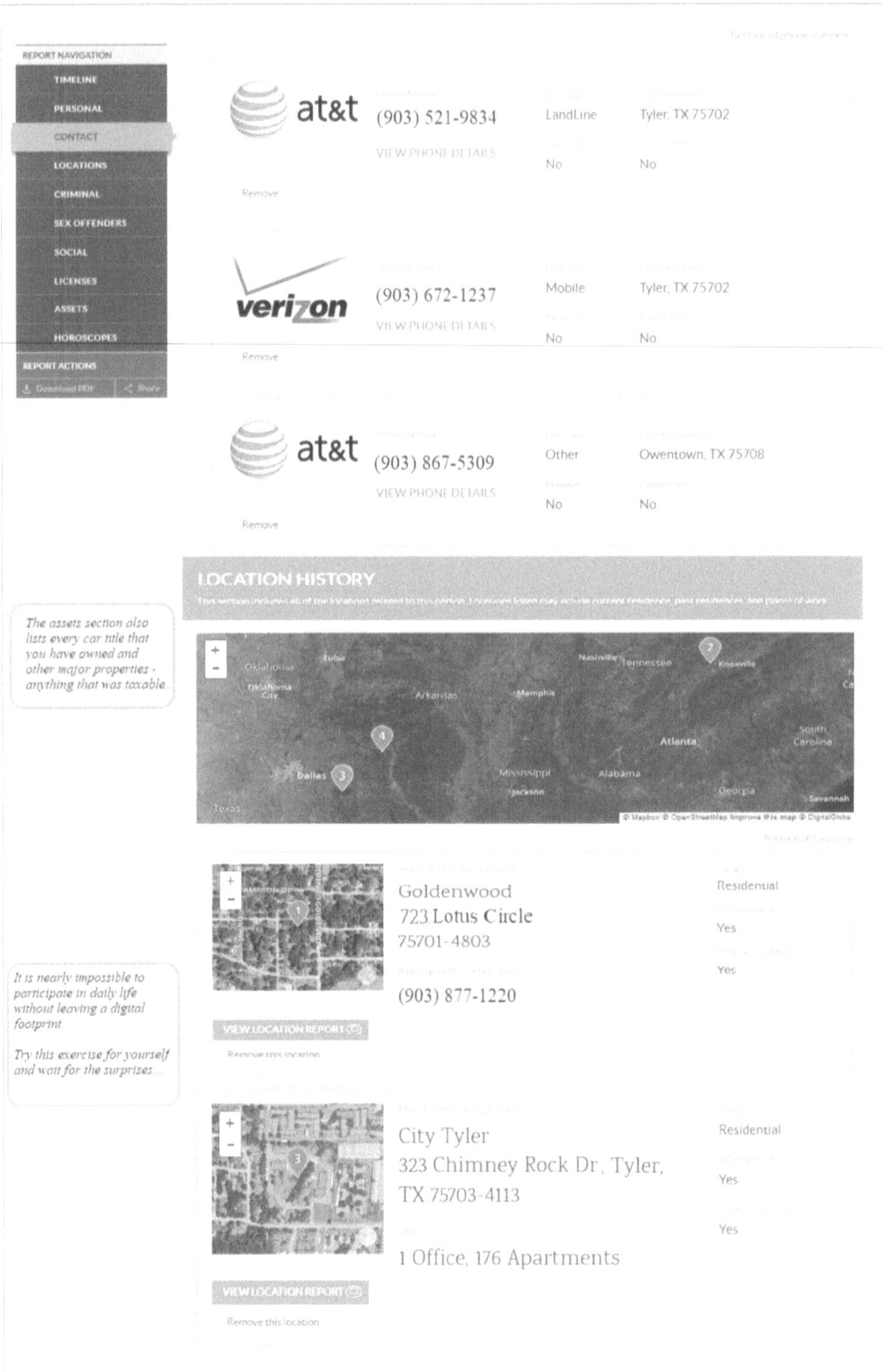

The assets section also lists every car title that you have owned and other major properties - anything that was taxable.

It is nearly impossible to participate in daily life without leaving a digital footprint.

Try this exercise for yourself and wait for the surprises...

Index

Page references for figures and tables are italicized.

About the Authors

Raised around his dad's radio/TV business and taking his first distance course by television in the third grade, **Mickey Slimp** has always felt close to technology. Funding a humanities degree with work in video production and then as an on-the-air journalist, he found his direction covering striking coal mine politics on the Kentucky/Tennessee/Virginia border. Identifying effective communication and improved schools as solutions to the rural dilemma, he pursued his advanced degrees in rural settings, studying change theory and educational technology.

Along the way, he completed a dissertation on educational technology in Belize, designed telecourses and other media at two Texas A&M branch campuses, and followed with a brief stint on a virtual lab simulation team at the Auburn University College of Veterinary Medicine. Returning to Texas, he built a nationally recognized distance learning program as a dean at Tyler Junior College. He was the founding director of the Virtual College of Texas, chaired the Instructional Technology Council of the American Association of Community Colleges (AACC), and served on an AACC commission.

For the past 15 years, he has led the Northeast Texas Consortium of Colleges and Universities, with a mission to "increase access to education and healthcare for the rural citizens of the region through collaboration and advanced technology" (https://www.netnet.org/). He serves on the Internet2 Community Anchor Network's national advisory board and has been inducted into the Texas Distance Learning Association's Hall of Fame.

The Northeast Texas Consortium is based at the University of Texas Health Science Center at Tyler, where Dr. Slimp also serves as the associate provost for student support.

After three decades of work in technology and technology-related fields, **Roy Bartels** retired from Western Texas College as chief technology and information security officer. He first began working with computers in the late 1980s, when personal computers were first gaining in popularity. In the early years, he developed and presented training for proprietary and nonproprietary applications, helping companies such as Metromedia Paging, PageNet, Southwestern Bell, Pac*Tel, GTE, and Raytheon with training and development needs. He entered higher education in 2004, quickly moving into administration.

Roy served on the Learning Technology Advisory Council of the Texas Higher Education Coordinating Board, the board of the Instructional Technology Council, and the West Texas Telecommunications Council (of the Region 14 Education Service Center, Texas Education Agency). He helped manage four federal grants, all of which helped improve technology on campus to the benefit of faculty, staff, and students. He holds a master of education degree in educational technology from the University of Texas at Brownsville, a bachelor of music in education degree from Southwestern University, and two certificates in distance education from the University of Wisconsin–Madison. In 2018, he received the Vice Chancellor's Award in Excellence from Texas A&M University.

www.ingramcontent.com/pod-product-compliance
Ingram Content Group UK Ltd.
Pitfield, Milton Keynes, MK11 3LW, UK
UKHW012040150926
475560UK00001B/111